Sail

...this way.

A plain guide to ocean sailing.

Stuart MacDonald

By the same author: The Long Way Home.

www.beyondsailing.com

For all who sail and for all who long to.

With thanks to Anna MacDonald for the cover design and to Christine Fyfe, partner and sailing companion, for her endless patience.

FOREWORD

The opinions I express in this book and the suggestions I make regarding the various ways of doing things, are my own. They have evolved over many years of being at sea, both on merchant vessels and sailing yachts. They may not reflect current teaching at formal sailing schools, but they have worked for me.

There is a difference between being very experienced at doing something and being very good at it.

After all the years I have spent sailing, and the thousands of miles I have covered, I think I can claim to be in the first category, and possibly the second. That said, despite a few near misses, I am, at least, still here and more or less in one piece.

Perhaps I just got lucky.

Stuart MacDonald.

May 2017.

BEYOND.

Resting in New Zealand.

CONTENTS

1. MY FRIEND THE SEA.

Why go sailing anyway?

Regulation is creeping into our daily lives like rising damp, as governments and other authorities impose rules which they say are in our best interests.

Sailing the oceans is one of the last real freedoms left. Crossing thousands of miles of water, driven along by the wind and kept safe by your own common sense and self-reliance is a fabulous and fulfilling experience.

Alone at sea, you are responsible to no one, and for no one, other than yourself. You can make your own rules, then decide whether you stick to them or not. You can stand up, lie down, sleep, shout, whistle, sing, dance or snore as you wish. You may wear what clothes you wish, or none at all if that suits you better. You are free. Free to sail, free to think and to dream. At one stage of my four year voyage around the world I went for two years without reading a newspaper or watching television. It didn't seem to do me any harm.

You can decide whether to communicate with other boats or friends ashore, or not. It's up to you. You can decide when and what to eat and when to have a drink, whether or not to keep the boat and yourself in good shape, clean and working efficiently, or not. It's up to you.

On passage, if you do not like the time the sun rises or sets, you can change the clocks on board to suit yourself. On a two thousand mile East West passage you have plenty of flexibility and if you arrive half an hour out of step with the country you arrive in, so what? Change them back again.

Travelling this way you can be your own master, and master of your little world. Being on a small boat, a thousand miles from the nearest land, is true reality. You deal with whatever the wind and the sea hands out, good and bad. How you do it is up to you.

This little book is not designed to teach you to sail; it assumes a certain degree of knowledge. My hope is that, having read it, you will feel more confident in setting off on longer passages, and if you do, that the information and advice the book contains will help keep you safe, and in doing so increase your enjoyment of the experience.

2. THE CRUISING LIFE.

LONG AND SHORT TERM SAILING LIFESTYLES.

There is a quite marked distinction between the culture which prevails amongst those cruising for a relatively short time, possibly a few months or a year, and those who are in it for the long haul. I think this is because for the short term cruiser, living at home is the norm and life on the boat is the exception. For the long-term sailors, it becomes the other way around. You live on board, and occasionally think of home. Just as when you are on holiday you probably go out more, drink more and stay up later than you would at home, the longer term sailors, the 'live-aboards', tend to lead a quieter life than those on a short summer cruise.

For me the transition between lifestyles became very apparent at the Panama Canal. I had just spent a few months in the Caribbean, resting after my Atlantic crossing and having a lot of fun, surrounded by other boats who had made the same trip and were similarly relaxing. Many of the boats were equipped with the best of everything and many of the people were clearly from a world of overt sailing consumerism. A walk along the pontoon was rather like going to a boat show or lifestyle event, with children in the very best of kit, tearing along on shiny scooters with their lap tops in their back packs. It may not have been as opulent as St. Tropez, but there weren't many people saving up for their next pair of socks.

In Panama, the scene changes. Boats going through the canal which are starting their cruising lives are committing to something big. Once you are through that canal, it's a little like strapping on a parachute and jumping out of a plane for the first time. You just hope it's all going to be ok, because for sure, there's no way back. Many of the boats you meet at the canal will have started their journeys years previously, in New Zealand, Australia or South Africa, and will be heading home, already completely immersed in the cruising life. Things are quieter and more relaxed, with faded T shirts, battered hats and bare feet being the norm. Here, surrounded by these very experienced, relaxed and friendly folk, I realised that whilst I had come a fair way from Scotland, my adventure was just beginning. I was a relative newcomer to the world of long term cruising and I still had a lot to learn.

PEOPLE.

The people you meet, both on other boats and ashore are one of the most memorable things about a long cruise. Ocean cruising people, sometimes referred to as voyagers, are united by the common experience of having crossed oceans and covered long distances under sail, a mode of transport generally discarded by those in the know as wholly impractical about a century ago. This experience generates a largely shared outlook and provides a very good basis on which to build new friendships. Because ocean cruising routes and timings are, in general, dictated by the seasons, the same group of boats may meet up with each other again and again over months and years as they make their way along the same well-trodden cruising routes. As a downwind ocean voyager you will become part of this itinerant floating population of like-minded ocean gypsies. It's a great family to be part of and like most families, has its own conventions, largely unspoken.

VISITING OTHER BOATS.

You should never make your dinghy fast to another yacht you do not know, without first hailing the occupants, or perhaps knocking on the hull, if they are alongside. They can then either chat with you, as you sit in the dinghy, or invite you aboard, should they wish to do so, and don't step from the dock, or out of a dinghy onto another boat without first removing your shoes, unless of course it's very cold. Nearly all your trade wind cruising will be in warm weather and you will be in flip flops, or already barefoot anyway.

If the weather is good and you are invited on board, expect to remain in the cockpit. Evening gatherings in the cockpits of neighbouring boats are a nightly occurrence. Although dark, the evenings are still warm and on cruising yachts nearly all socialising is done outside. The interior of a cruising boat is a home. It would be quite unusual to be invited below on a first visit, and certainly considered quite rude to ask to see down below.

If I am invited to visit another boat for drinks, whether I know the folk on board or not, I never arrive empty handed. You can't expect to step onto someone else's boat and sit and consume their beer all evening without making some sort of contribution, although I have seen it done.

CRUISERS MIDNIGHT.

A lot of your cruising will be done in tropical latitudes where it gets dark early, often not long after six. This encourages people to turn in early, to take advantage of the cool of the evening to sleep. We used to call nine o'clock Cruisers Midnight.

A great deal of pleasure can be had by rising early in an anchorage, and I have spent many peaceful and happy times sitting in the cockpit with a mug of tea, listening to the sounds of life starting up ashore and seeing the smoke begin to rise from the huts and small houses along the beach. To lie at anchor in some Pacific lagoon after a long voyage and to hear dogs begin to bark and roosters crow as the sky lightens and the sun begins to rise is a wonderful experience.

LOCAL VISITORS.

Be very wary of inviting anyone you do not know onto your boat, particularly children. Often kids or adults will gather on the quay and look down at the boat and start up a conversation. That's fine, but if they come on board you may find it very difficult to get rid of them again. That's particularly true if you are anchored and they have arrived by boat or have swum out. In some areas of the Pacific it is quite common, and not considered at all rude, for local people visiting to simply pick up something of yours and say "Give me this". Start doing that and you will be on a slippery slope.

SHOWING THE FLAG.

Cruising is a very international affair and most cruising boats are a long way from home. It is always good practice to fly the ensign of your country, particularly when arriving in an anchorage for the first time, when you may not be known to the other yachts already there. A cruising yacht may have crew members on board from countries other than that in which the yacht is registered, and many will fly a small national flag of their crew's country from their port spreaders. It's a custom which I rather dismissed at first, but one I came to like very much, and although I always flew a Red Ensign from the stern I also flew the Saint Andrew's cross of Scotland from the port spreader. The starboard spreader is of course, reserved for the courtesy flag of the country you are visiting. When I had crew on board of another nationality, I flew their ensign below the Scottish one, which gives other boats an indication of the languages being spoken on board. I was always pleased to see another boat with a Scottish flag at their spreader, and when I also flew the Argentinian flag, we would frequently have other Spanish speaking cruisers come over for a chat. It's a great ice-breaker and can lead to many a spontaneous social gathering.

There are a number of clubs which cater mainly to cruising yachts, such as the Cruising Association and the Ocean Cruising Club. I am a member of the latter and I always flew the Club burgee when in port. It's surprising how often boats belonging to fellow members of these clubs will meet by chance in some far flung location. Like nationality, membership tends to provide a mutual bond. I greatly enjoyed meeting up with other members of the OCC as I made my way around the world.

WELCOME.

A yacht arriving in an anchorage such as the harbour in Rodriguez, or in the Cocos Islands, will have spent a long time at sea, and her people will probably be very glad to get in. If you have been there for a while, you will probably already have managed to get hold of a few luxuries like fresh bread or milk. If you know the people on board the new arrival it's a nice gesture to row over, once they have their anchor set, and ask them if there is anything they need, and perhaps to hand over a loaf and some fresh milk.

When I arrived in Rodriguez after a really tough passage across the Indian Ocean from Cocos Keeling, I was dead beat. I got into the lagoon at about nine in the morning and tied alongside the harbour wall where a few boats I knew who had left Cocos earlier than I were already moored. Norwegian friends shouted hello and within five minutes I was enjoying a great breakfast in their cockpit, complete with cold beer. Expressions of friendship mean a great deal at times like that.

A few days later I heard that a relatively small Swiss boat I knew was going to arrive. I knew they would be worn out. They anchored off the pier and I rowed over with some bread and fresh stuff, which they were very pleased to get. Is there anything else I can get for you? I asked.

"Cigarettes and wine!"

THE VISITORS BOOK.

It's a good idea to keep a boat visitors book. You can of course decide whether or not you ask other sailors who visit to sign it. It is very pleasant to look back over the years and the ports you have visited, and remember the people you met along the way. Mine has some truly memorable and amusing entries, which still raise a smile years after they were penned. It's also a pleasure to be asked to sign another boat's book.

BOAT CARDS.

Boat cards are just like business cards, but with the boat's name usually taking prominence, followed by the name of the owner. Many long distance cruising boats have a crew of two, and their names are usually shown along with the boat's home port, and her call sign. Often the background will be a picture of the boat. These cards are also very useful when visiting an office ashore, such as customs or immigration, where English may not be the first language.

THE CRUISERS NET.

In ports or anchorages where cruising boats gather in numbers, such as Prickly Bay in Grenada and other well frequented spots around the world it is common to have an established cruisers' VHF radio net in place, which usually operates first thing each morning. There will be one boat designated as net controller, and they will do the job for a week or so, then hand over to another.

Typically the net controller will begin by calling for any boat with problems or emergencies which have occurred during the previous night to come on the air and report. Happily there are normally none and the controller will move on to relay the weather forecast, and any items of local news that the assembled boats should know about.

New arrivals will be invited to introduce themselves and those planning to leave that day will say goodbye and give details of their next destination.

The net then deals with non-urgent problems, and local service providers ashore, all of whom have VHF radios, will come on to talk about special deals, etc.

After that the net tends to slide into a morass of trivia and inter-boat banter. In the Caribbean anchorages there is often a group of lady cruising sailors who seem intent on re-creating small town America amongst the assembled fleet, with their talk of doughnut bake-ins, yoga groups and so on.

I usually switch off at that point, but in general the net is a great idea and serves a very useful purpose.

WHEN ASHORE.

Very few of the cruising people you will meet will be wealthy, or certainly not overtly so. Cruising is a very simple existence and whilst some people will have more funds behind them than others, it would certainly be unusual to see anyone making a display of splashing money around.

However, you have to remember that in many of the places you visit, particularly the more isolated ones, you will be considered to be very wealthy indeed by the locals. Quite apart from anything else, you have a yacht and whilst at times this might seem like a financial burden to you, to others it is a clear sign of great prosperity. If only they knew…

So when you are in places that enjoy a very simple lifestyle, such as some of the Pacific Islands where mainstream tourism does not exist, avoid walking around with cameras worth hundreds of dollars on display, and an expensive watch on your wrist. Try and blend in.

If you are visiting a small village, such as those you find in the Yasawas in Fiji, or in Vanuatu, always ask permission before you take photographs. These villages are sometimes quite haphazard in their layout, without any fences or boundary walls such as we are accustomed to and it would be quite wrong just to wander around amongst the huts. It would be like someone walking into your garden at home, then wandering about without even asking permission. In Fiji it is customary to seek out the headman or chief of the village and ask his permission to land and visit. He will often assign one of his men to be your guide. This is a longstanding tradition dating back to the days when strangers were often potential enemies. When the chief gives his permission to visit, tradition dictates that you come under his protection for as long as you remain within his village. The downside is that should he decide to go to war with another island while you are there, the same tradition will require you to pick up your club and join in. Thankfully I always seemed to arrive in peaceful times. Whatever you do, always be courteous and respectful. Don't become a nuisance to the locals. If a situation seems at all awkward, withdraw politely and go back aboard. I went ashore at Ambryn Island in Vanuatu and walked through the trees up a track from the beach. I came into a small collection of huts. It was mid-morning, but the only sign of life was the presence of a couple of pigs rooting about under the trees. I realised that the people who lived there had seen me coming and were watching me from inside their houses. I turned round and went back to the boat.

Respect local tradition and conventions. In some countries it is considered very bad form to wear scanty clothing, or to consume alcohol in public. This does not, of course, apply in the Caribbean where near naked inebriation seems to be the accepted norm in many beach resorts. But the Caribbean is not representative of the wonderful cruising areas which lie to the West.

In Tonga, for instance, you are not permitted to engage in any sort of sporting activity, to swim or sing or dance on a Sunday. Nor are you allowed to play a musical instrument, other than to accompany hymns. Even smiling is frowned upon. The harbourmaster broadcasts a reminder about this on VHF each Saturday, and all the visiting boats respect the custom. Peace and quiet prevail.

PAY UP.

I always made it a point of paying yard dues and other boat bills as soon as the work was done and the bill was produced. Word gets around if you don't, and you will soon find yourself unable to get any help at all if you get the reputation of being someone who has to be chased for payment.

Never sail out of a port owing money, you will just be making it very tough for the next boat that comes along and needs something done. Leave a clean wake, in all respects. Those you leave behind should always be pleased to see you back again. In the Pacific, and on the North coast of Australia, I came across a few boats lying derelict. Their owners had found themselves owing money, the boat had been abandoned to rot where it lay, and they had gone home, their cruising dreams at an end.

3. A FEW FORMALITIES.

ARRIVAL FORMALITIES.

Unless you are arriving from a port within the same national jurisdiction as that of your destination, such as a European yacht does when arriving from another European country, you will have to go through the process known as "Clearing Inwards". That is, you will have to be checked and cleared by Port Health, Immigration and Customs. These authorities have absolute power, and you must comply with all of the regulations they impose, no matter how frustrating or pointless they appear to you. You must take these formalities seriously and treat the officials involved with courtesy. You are, after all, arriving and asking to stay in their country. Port Health can refuse you permission to land, Immigration can do the same, and possibly deport you as well. Customs authorities have absolute right of entry to and inspection of every last nook and cranny of your boat, and of you. If you don't believe me, sail to Australia, New Zealand or South Africa and try and get smart with the authorities. Not every port is a port of entry, and you must make sure that your first arrival is at one that is.

Certain countries such as Australia and New Zealand require you to submit advanced notice of arrival, which you can do via email. These countries have some of the strictest rules and entry procedures of anywhere in the world and there are many tales of how tough they can be. In fact I found the authorities in both countries to be friendly and very helpful indeed.

21

In South Africa, I was required to go through the full procedure at every port I arrived at then left from, even though they were all within South Africa, and to file a "flight plan" with the authorities every time I set off to sail down the coast to my next port. It was a complete pain, but it had to be done.

Let's deal with Port Health first of all.

FREE PRATIQUE.

Historically, other than as a result of the movement of marching armies, infectious diseases such as the plague, or yellow fever were usually carried from one country to another by sea. Any vessel arriving from foreign lands was required to pass health checks before her people were allowed ashore or she was allowed to work cargo. On arrival, she would fly the yellow Q flag, if she believed there had been no signs of having plague or other infectious disease on board. In the days of trading under sail, when there was no radio communication the first knowledge a port authority would have had of a ship's arrival would probably be when she turned up and anchored off the port.

Seeing the Q flag, a doctor would board and check for signs of disease. The captain was required to report any cases of disease or to sign a declaration to the effect that there had been no sign of plague, such as an unusually high rate of mortality amongst the rats on board (always a bad sign) and answer various other relevant questions. Presumably a few of the ship's company dying on the trip would also have been seen as an indication of a potential problem, but as I recall from my days as a ship's Captain, the question regarding the rats was higher up the list.

These days when cruise ships turn up on tight schedules and thousands of passengers pour ashore the formalities have been streamlined, but they persist in principle. It all seems a little pointless compared with the airline industry when hundreds of thousands of passengers jet back and forward from one country to another on a daily basis. They, of course, can have contracted something unpleasant in one country and then spent weeks in another before they even realise they are ill, but that's progress I suppose.

But, back to the reality of life on your sailing boat. On arrival from another country you must always fly Flag Q, usually on the starboard side below the courtesy flag and you must continue to fly it until you have completed all the formalities. In some countries you will not be allowed to come alongside until this has been done. In others, such as Australia and New Zealand your boat will be directed to a quarantine area, or alongside a quarantine pontoon, with no shore access, where officials will board and carry out their checks. In areas such as the Caribbean, where there are islands within a day's sail of each other, which belong to different countries, procedures are of necessity more relaxed because of the high number of boats moving around within the island groups. In some cases it is possible to go to the marina office and check in and out online.

IMMIGRATION.

Whilst Port Health are concerned with whether or not you pose a health threat, Immigration are concerned with who you and your crew are, and whether or not you have the right to enter their country. They will require a crew list, showing the full names of everyone on board, their nationality and place and date of birth and they will want to see everyone's passport. They will then issue a visa and give each person a limited length of time during which they may remain in the country. As skipper you are responsible for everyone on board and for making sure that they obey the rules and depart on time. Depending on how well you know your crew it may be a good idea to keep control of all the passports. Immigration officials may require you to visit their offices ashore rather than boarding the boat. If so, you need to take all the passports with you, but not all of the people. Some countries require you to send advance copies of the information relating to the crew by email. Being single-handed most of the time, this was never a problem for me.

If a crew member is planning to leave the boat, and then the country, on an air ticket, you may be required to produce the ticket, and you will certainly have to report to the Immigration office and have their departure noted, before they head for the airport.

It's a good idea to have plenty of blank crew lists made up, and to have a ship's stamp made, to authenticate your signature as captain. You can easily create a formal looking list on a printer, with the boat's name, registered number and port of registry at the top, and space at the foot for your signature as captain and the date. Add the imprint of the ship's stamp and the document starts to look pretty good, certainly better than a page torn from a notebook with some spidery biro handwriting on it. A boat that presents something like that is basically saying that they don't take the process seriously. That is never a good starting point, no matter what you are doing.

In some areas such as French Polynesia, there has been a historic problem with yacht crew moving ashore and overstaying their visas, or of skippers and their boats running out of funds and being unable to depart. Understandably, the authorities do not like this, and depending on the nationality of your crew members, you may be required to post a financial bond sufficient to cover the cost of their repatriation. The bond is recoverable on departure.

In Fiji and in some other countries, if a member of the crew leaves the boat and enters the country illegally, you as skipper will be held responsible. Under these circumstances you absolutely must retain all the passports because handing over the passport of a crew member who has absconded is your stay out of jail card.

Everyone on board should have a few colour copies of the ID page of their passport made, and keep one them with them always.

CUSTOMS.

Whilst Immigration are concerned with who is on board, Customs are concerned with what is on board. It is an unfortunate fact that there have been many instances of yachts carrying illegal substances and Customs are naturally keen to catch the offenders. On arrival you will be required to present your outwards clearance from the last port visited, (see the section on Departure) and the boat's certificate of registry in order to satisfy the authorities that she is the vessel named in the clearance document. It is not necessary to have a full Part 1 Certificate of Registry, a Small Ships Registry Certificate is sufficient. You will also have to fill out a declaration giving the exact amounts of tobacco, spirits, beer, cigarettes, etc, on board, and to sign a statement to the effect that the boat is not carrying any illegal substances. Customs officers are very experienced at assessing the likelihood of a boat and her skipper trying to break the rules, and they have absolute authority to search the boat from top to bottom and if they feel so inclined, to take it apart. That's worth remembering, because they are not required to put it back together again. They are also empowered to arrest the boat and detain her … and you.

Having said that, apart from one occasion on which a sniffer dog was brought on board, Beyond was never the subject of anything more than a cursory inspection and I always found Customs people to be easy to deal with. Perhaps I just looked like a rather dull sort of guy with no bad habits.

I was nearly always on my own and never did carry wine, spirits, tobacco or cigarettes on board anyway. To add to that I was almost always nearly out of beer on arrival, and the very low level of my stock of stores and the complete absence of anything more exciting than a couple of beers was the subject of frequent amusement amongst Customs boarding officers. When I first arrived in New Zealand, it was in the evening and even after the formalities I was not allowed to move from the quarantine dock until the next morning. The very strict entry procedure had included handing over all items of fresh food, dairy produce and meat. That done, the Customs guys, who were most friendly and courteous, looked at my almost empty lockers and my three cans of Tongan lager, and shook their heads. "Is that it Captain?" "That's it."

"Ah well, have a great night!"

DEPARTURE.

Before sailing from one country to another you will be required to clear outwards. This will involve visits to Customs and Immigration, but rarely Port Health. I suppose if you have caught something unpleasant during your visit they will be quite happy to get rid of you.

Customs will want you to declare that you are not exporting anything illegal, and, if you have shipped stores such as tobacco and alcohol at duty free prices, they will check that you have not exceeded your allowance. They will also need to satisfy themselves that the goods are actually leaving on your boat, and that you have not shipped them at the duty free price then sold them for profit. Any local supplier such as a boatyard to whom you might owe money, or anyone else who has a claim on the boat can inform the Customs who will not allow you to leave until the matter is settled.

Immigration will check that everyone who was on board when you arrived is leaving on the boat, or if not, that there is a paper trail to demonstrate that they have been allowed to stay, or have left the country already by some other means.

If all is well, you will be given an outwards clearance document. This is your permission to go, and your proof to the authorities in the next country that you visit that you sailed in good order, in accordance with all the rules and that you left no bad debt behind you. Cruising boats often leave in groups, and it may be that the authorities are issuing clearance documents to several boats at more or less the same time. Confusion can arise. Check your clearance document to make sure that the details are correct, and that it is the one that applies to your boat. Arriving at the next place with a clearance document which applies to another yacht can be awkward. Once you have checked it, put it somewhere safe and look after it carefully until it is time to present it to the authorities at the next port you visit.

Most clearance documents have a limited lifespan, often 24 hours, within which time you must leave, or go through the whole process again. In Fiji, you must leave immediately. The day I left I attended the Customs office in Lautoka at eight in the morning and checked out. They wanted to put a Customs man in the dinghy with me so that he could come aboard and search the boat for stowaways. However, when they took into account the size of their man and the size of my partially deflated dinghy they changed their minds. Nonetheless, they watched me board, secure the dinghy and depart. It wasn't that they had taken a particular dislike to me or the boat, that was just the way it was.

If you leave without permission and without a clearance, the port authorities are very likely to pursue you and force you to return. This will probably be done by the coastguard who will take delight in enforcing the order and may be less than gentle about it.

If you leave with a clearance, and have to turn back as a result of some problem or other, you must report in again. If you do not, you will be in big trouble. In 2011 I completed departure formalities and left Tonga for New Zealand, but had to turn back because of lack of wind. Instead of going into the port I had left, I anchored off a nearby island and hid for a few days. The weather turned bad and I had to go back into the harbour. When the Customs guys realised what I had done, I was in very big trouble indeed and lucky to escape a heavy fine.

It's just not worth taking chances.

SOME GENERAL STUFF.

Make copies of all the documents relevant to the boat and keep them in a safe place.

Keep all the originals in a folder, so that you can present them to whichever official needs to see them without having to scrabble and fumble around looking for some missing bit of paper.

When you are going to visit the offices of Customs, Health or Immigration ashore, dress properly; you are after all going to a government office and not to a barbecue.

If officials are to board the boat, make sure you have all the ship's papers, passports, etc, ready for them. Dress properly, be polite, smile and answer all the questions.

Do not argue, it is never worth it. The people you are talking to did not make the rules, they are there to enforce them and it will all go much more smoothly if you allow them to do so without making life difficult.

4. WEAR AND TEAR.

GETTING READY.

The average marina based cruising boat, sailing at weekends and with one summer cruise, may do around one thousand miles a year, over a six month season. Many don't do anywhere near that.

The average ocean cruiser, without a lay-up season, will do much more. In the final year of Beyond's circumnavigation she covered over ten thousand miles. I think it's not unreasonable to apply a factor of seven, when comparing the amount of wear a boat will experience in one year of voyaging compared to her marina based sister. In addition, the miles are being done in open water, with its greater swell and wave heights, imposing constant cyclical movement on the boat and her rig over long periods.

There are things on board which are designed to move, like the gooseneck, the connections between the kicker and its brackets on the mast and on the boom, the rudder bearings or pintles, the wheel bearings and linkages in the steering system and so on, and they move constantly. Movement between surfaces causes wear, and as the play in a connection, such as the gooseneck, starts to exceed the designed limit, the rate of wear increases. Things which should turn or move smoothly start to rattle and clunk and the situation gets rapidly worse. Things that should move, move more, and things that shouldn't move often start to. Noise is often the first sign that this is happening, and as a general rule, clunking and creaking are nearly always bad news.

Here are a few things to think about before you set off.

Think about a boat reaching in a quartering sea and ocean swell, in moderate weather. As she rolls and dips, the loads on the boom and its connections alternately rise, fall and reverse direction many times a minute, hundreds of times an hour and thousands of times a day. Think of this going on for a couple of weeks at a time, and you can see what I mean. It is worth bracing the boom forward with a fore-guy and sideways as well, immobilising it as far as possible. More about this in the section where we deal with the rig.

When you are thinking of getting the boat ready it's a good idea to first make a list of absolutely everything on the boat that moves and will wear, then check the level of existing wear on all of it. If you are in the least doubt, replace the item. I would go as far as to say that if the boat is five years old, or older and you have no note of any of these things having been replaced already, you should replace them anyway, because they will wear out within a year or so, and possibly break, just when the boat is in some location where you are unable to repair or replace them. It's a good idea to carry a spare set of pins for the gooseneck and kicker brackets and a spare set of bearings for the rudder and the wheel steering mechanism. Check the size of the rivets on the kicker and gooseneck brackets, they will probably be 8 mm, which may not be readily available overseas, so get a full set of spares, and a man-sized set of rivet tongs as well.

The bearings on the top horizontal pinion of a wheel-steered boat take a lot of wear, because most helmsmen tend to exert backwards pressure on the top of the wheel when they are steering in waves. To check for wear, stand behind the wheel and try to move the top of the wheel backwards and forwards. If it moves, there is wear on the bearings and possibly the pinion. The bearings are usually protected by a water seal, and are vulnerable if the seal goes. Spare seals and bearings are a good bet. If the connection to the rudder stock is via a line or chain, replace the connection and carry a spare set of chains or wires. If the connection is via a solid rod, replace the rod end ball joints and carry a couple of spares. While you are at it, check the movement on the gas line to the stove, to see if it wears against anything when the stove swings through the full arc of its gimbals. Finally, check the pins on which the stove sits in its gimbals. Mine failed in bad weather North of Australia, and the stove set off across the boat in the middle of the night. Not much fun. I managed to secure it with some bits of wood and a sail tie, but it didn't swing anymore and I spent the last couple of days of the trip holding the kettle and the pan on to the gas if I wanted anything to eat or drink.

I replaced as many shackles as I could with Spectra or Dyneema lashings, including those attaching the mainsheet blocks to the boom. The clew of the mainsail was attached to the outhaul eye by a shackle, and also to the car which held it down on to the boom. All of these metal to metal contacts rattle and click in light weather when there's a sea and quite apart from the wear this causes, the noise can be a dreadful irritation. I replaced the shackles with soft Spectra lashings. Take a look at any modern ocean-racing boat, you won't see many shackles. It's a good idea to check every bearing surface and connection before you set off on a long passage. Eliminate metal to metal contact wherever possible. Nip up shackle pins with the key or a pair of piers. I had a Saturday routine for this sort of thing when I was on a voyage.

Sails which are trimmed in hard, such as when going to windward, or on a shy reach, rarely chafe against anything, particularly if the wind is steady and fresh. The chafe problem arises when the sheets are eased, because this mean the sails touch something harder than themselves, such as the pulpit in the case of a jib, or on the spreader end in the case of the mainsail. Not only that, because the sail is eased, it can move up and down as well as in and out, the sail will not just bear on the harder surface, it will move back and forwards over it and rub against it every time the boat moves. If the jib is eased on to a reach, the sheet will almost certainly rub against the top lifeline. The same foot or two of the sheet will move out and in across the wire, and back and forwards along it. The bigger the swell or sea, the more the sheet will move over the wire. It all sounds very obvious to anyone who has sailed at all, but you will be amazed at the amount of chafe you will get in a week of reaching in a big sea. Beyond has swept back spreaders so the sail tends to bear quite sharply against the spreader ends. I have parcelled them heavily with leather and I have put a plastic tube on the section of the top rail over which the eased jib sheet runs.

Mark the point on the sail that bears on the spreader and stick on spreader patches. Look at where the batten pockets touch the shrouds. Double the thickness on the pockets at the places where they touch. I used stick on Kevlar cloth. Then take in each reef in turn and repeat the process. You will end up with a selection of patches on the sail, but that's much better than a selection of holes in it. I prefer to stick the patches on, rather than sew them, because it's easier to replace them when they wear, and if they are doing their job they certainly will. Sail downwind and ease the mainsheet right off, with the kicker hard on, and see if the sheet bears against anything, such as the rear edge of the spray hood. If it does, figure out a way of preventing damage.

It's impossible to eliminate wear altogether if you are going to sail long distances, but a little forethought and attention to the kind of things I have been talking about before you set off will certainly help. You are sure to discover more as your trip progresses.

5. DINGHIES AND OUTBOARDS.

Yachts on an extended cruise spend far more time at anchor than alongside. The simple reason for this is that in many of the areas they will visit, there are no marina facilities or harbours where it is possible to lie alongside.

When Beyond sailed from Panama to New Zealand, a trip which took over six months, she spent 118 nights at anchor, and only 10 nights alongside. Being at anchor becomes second nature and many cruisers much prefer it to being alongside. There is greater security, and less likelihood of unwelcome visitors. Many Pacific harbours are pretty rough and dirty places and there is very little pleasure in lying alongside a pontoon or harbour wall at night and watching rats and cockroaches scuttling about.

At anchor, the boat becomes your out of town cottage, and your dinghy becomes the transport you use every day, to head in to town or to visit other boats. The dinghy gets worked very hard.

DINGHIES.

I suppose the first choice is whether to have a rigid floor, an inflatable floor, or a soft floor with slats or boards. Rigid floor dinghies have big advantages in terms of being able to carry load and, with a sufficiently powerful outboard, to plane. But cruising is supposed to be a leisurely business, and whilst a planing dinghy will be a real advantage on a bigger yacht where there are multiple trips being made back and forwards with crew, guests and so on, the great majority of cruising yachts of forty feet and under do not carry a dinghy that planes.

If you are sitting quietly amongst other yachts in an anchorage, there is something quite intrusive about a dinghy which repeatedly planes back and forward through the anchorage, making noise and creating wash. I often wondered why these folk needed to go everywhere at top speed.

A rigid floor dinghy cannot, of course be rolled up or folded away. So you need space on deck or a set of davits in which to stow the dinghy. If I had a boat that was long enough to have a dinghy stowed on deck, or a boat with davits, I would certainly have a rigid floored dinghy. But I don't.

So if you are like most cruising boats I met on my journey, you will go for a soft bottomed dinghy with a solid transom, and slatted floor pieces, or with an inflatable floor.

You can pay an awful lot of money for a high-end dinghy, but I don't think it's necessary, and I will talk about that later in this chapter.

OUTBOARDS.

For a three metre soft floor dinghy, usually carrying two or three people, you can get by perfectly well with a 2.5 HP outboard. You will not plane, of course, but there will be sufficient power to get you around in comfort.

Power means weight, and whilst a 2.5 HP motor is light enough to manhandle into and out of the dinghy, a 4.0 HP motor will be considerably heavier and will almost certainly need some sort of davit to handle it.

If you are going to have a rigid floor dinghy, you will almost certainly want a more powerful and therefore heavier outboard and whilst 4.0 HP might get you by, you would probably go for 9.0 HP or larger and accept the fact that the outboard will be heavier to handle. Engines of this size usually carry a remote fuel tank, which is something else you will have to lift in and out of the dinghy and stow.

So, if you are setting off on an average cruising boat below forty five feet, without davits, you will probably settle for a three metre dinghy with a 2.5 HP motor.

When looking for a small outboard, you can choose between air or water-cooled, and between two and four-stroke cycles.

There is little to choose between the two when it comes to weight. Two-stroke engines use an oil and petrol mixture, which powers the engine and lubricates the cylinder at the same time. You have to buy the oil and petrol and mix them yourself, in the correct ratio. It's not a big deal, just another small job that has to be done.

A four-stroke runs on straight petrol, and has its own oil reservoir, but because it has inlet and exhaust valves and an oil pump, it has more moving parts than the two-stroke.

A water-cooled engine with its sea water circulation system has more moving parts than an air-cooled motor, but will be quieter.

Outboard motors have advanced hugely over the last fifteen years and if looked after are extremely reliable.

I carried a 2.5 HP water-cooled, four-stroke motor, and although its outer cover became sun-bleached and some of the plastic fittings became brittle and broke, due to prolonged exposure to UV light, the internal mechanics of the engine operated faultlessly.

You need to be sure that the fuel you are using is absolutely clean. The carburettors on small outboards are small and very fiddly to work on, and if you get a build-up of dirty residue in the float chamber you will need to dismantle it and clean it out. Not an easy job. This happened to me on a couple of occasions, and looking back I should probably have drained the fuel system on the motor before I stowed it away in readiness for an ocean passage.

The only other thing that went wrong was that the rubber bush between the propeller hub and the drive shaft gave out, which meant that prop was slipping on the shaft and turning at fewer revs than the engine. Not good when trying to get out to the boat in a windy anchorage when you are taking the waves head on. On a few occasions I found myself on almost full revs making lots of noise and getting nowhere. I found that the answer was to keep the revs down and zig-zag across the waves.

I made a temporary repair by removing the prop, roughening up what was left of the bush and the inside of the hub with a file, smearing the whole thing in thickened epoxy and putting it back together.

It worked so successfully that when I finally got a spare prop in South Africa we had to cut the old one free with a disc grinder.

Other than these relatively minor problems the engine never let me down in five years of sometimes very rugged operation. It's still going strong.

SECURITY

Dinghies do get stolen. In the Caribbean, dinghy crime is rife and everyone chains their dinghy to the dock with a padlock. This might seem a bit sad, but who would leave a bicycle leaning unlocked against a lamp post for a day in any city and expect it to still be there when they got back?

There are lots of places where dinghy crime is not a problem, but, if you are in an area where it is, you should take a few elementary precautions:

Always keep the outboard padlocked to the dinghy, or to the boat itself when it is not in use.

Use a flexible stainless wire painter and padlock to secure the dinghy to the boat overnight.

Or, lift the dinghy clear of the water and secure it to the toe rail.

There is an argument for having a very tatty dinghy, on the basis that it will be less attractive to thieves than a shiny new one. There's a lot of sense in that argument. Some cruisers paint garish patterns on their dinghies to make them less attractive to thieves. Beyond's dinghy looked pretty good when I set off, but became distinctly rough looking over the following years, as did her outboard. As an aid to identification, I drilled a couple of ten millimetre holes in the wooden transom, and another two in the outboard casing, then photographed them. The thinking being that a thief could not easily hide these marks. The idea was never put to the test, but it may have worked as a deterrent because no one ever stole the boat.

In some Australian ports in the Northern Territories the local kids would steal dinghies off the beach, not for the boat itself, or for its motor, but to drain the petrol so that they could sniff it. A sad situation.

LIFTING ON BOARD.

I find the easiest way to get the dinghy aboard when at anchor is to put an overhand knot loop into the painter and attach a spare halyard to that. I then heave on the halyard. The yacht will probably be lying head to wind and with good timing, and a bit of luck, the dinghy will almost fly on board. Like most of these things, it looks great when it works!

I have never had davits, and I would not want to make a long sea passage, or try and manoeuvre in a windy marina with the windage of a dinghy hanging off the stern. Besides, a dinghy left inflated at the stern is constantly in the sun and will deteriorate far faster than one rolled up or stowed below decks.

STOWAGE.

Stowage options will be limited by the construction of the dinghy. Boats with a solid floor have many advantages but are, of course harder to stow on deck and take up more space. But, if you have a big enough yacht and can accommodate one, a rigid V-floored dinghy would be a great asset.

Because a dinghy with a slatted or an inflatable floor, can be rolled up when deflated, there are more stowage options available, such as in a locker, or tightly lashed on deck.

Unless the passage is short, say a couple of days, and in sheltered water, I always put the dinghy down in the locker. Getting it out can be an absolute pain, but I like to keep the coach roof clear when I am on passage. Also, if you do get into bad weather it's one less thing to worry about. On short trips it's tempting to be lazy and on Beyond I could deflate the bow section of the dinghy and then lash the half deflated boat between the mast and the sprayhood. I could then put the fenders and warps into the inflated portion, but with so much stuff on deck, the boat begins to look like a tinker's barrow and of course the dinghy catches all the rain and spray.

Unless the trip is very short indeed, say a few hours, I would not lash the dinghy upside down forward of the mast. It is vulnerable up there, creates windage where you don't want it and seriously restricts your ability to work on deck forward, and therefore your safety when doing so.

Stowage is closely linked to the subject of pumps.

PUMPS.

The easier it is to re-inflate the dinghy, the more inclined you will be to deflate it and stow it away properly.

A good dinghy inflation pump is worth its weight in gold. I started off with the usual foot bellows type, which slowly rotted during its prolonged spells in the locker when we were on passage. I well remember arriving in the Marquesas after three weeks at sea, tired and needing to lay out a stern anchor. I discovered that my pump had split along one of its rims and I had to spend a couple of hours bodging up a repair with glass cloth and epoxy before I could inflate the dinghy. Not a happy process.

In New Zealand I bought a vertical plunger type pump, and that worked very well, although there was a tendency for the top cover to pull off from the body of the pump, necessitating a lot of very fiddly reconstruction and the application of more epoxy around the top collar to try and stop it happening again. It wasn't until I got home and had a bit of spare cash that I bought an electric pump, which plugs into the 12V socket at the chart table. It has been great and I wish I had bought one years ago.

TOWING.

In New Zealand I would see yachts out in rough water on quite extended passages towing their dinghies but then Kiwis are a law unto themselves. For my part I never tow the dinghy on anything other than a sheltered passage, partly because it slows you down, but mainly because if the wind does get up to the point where the dinghy starts to misbehave, and shear about, it becomes very difficult to get it on board, particularly if you are on your own. I learned this the hard way as a young guy whilst sailing in the Orkney Islands. It became very windy very suddenly, as it does in those parts, and I had to try and get the dinghy aboard. As soon as the boat started to come clear of the water the wind got under it and it started to behave like some sort of demented kite. I was in real danger of being pulled over the side and at one point I thought I was going to have to cut the painter and let the boat go. Thankfully neither happened.

I never tow a dinghy on its painter. I always use a bridle, with the painter made fast, but lying slack between the boat and the dinghy. The bridle helps the dinghy to lie in a stable position and the painter acts as a safety line should the bridle fail. One last towing tip. Make sure the bridle and the painter are both made of floating rope, and when you are coming to anchor under engine, shorten the painter so that it can't go under the stern when you go astern on the engine. It seems obvious, but when you are coming to anchor all the attention is focussed on the bow and it's easy to forget the dinghy.

If the painter does find its way under the stern it has the choice of getting between the rudder and the hull, or round the prop, or both. Neither event will aid your smooth and professional looking arrival in the anchorage.

PAINTERS.

If you are going to land at a dinghy dock, you will often find that there are lots of dinghies already there, over which you will probably have to clamber to get ashore.

Make sure the painter is long enough to reach, and if you are there early enough and able to get ashore directly, leave a long painter. That way others coming after you can move your dinghy out of the way without untying it. If I am in an area where it's advisable to padlock the dinghy, I use a long length of flexible stainless wire with a soft eye in each end. I carried a selection of these, of different lengths. Having soft eyes means that you can easily join two or more together to increase the overall length. They are also useful for securing the dinghy to the boat when you shut down for the night.

DINGHY ANCHOR.

I carry a small collapsible grapnel style anchor in the dinghy. It can be very useful if the outboard quits in a windy anchorage when you are halfway between the boat and the shore, or to hold the dinghy in position whilst you swim or snorkel. I have the anchor line knotted every five metres, so that I can use the anchor as a sounding lead. It's very useful if you want to explore and check the depth for an anchoring spot close inshore.

THINGS THAT WORE OUT.

No matter how careful you are with it, your dinghy will take a beating. When it's not baking in the sun, or getting soaked with salt water, it gets stood on, dragged up beaches, and hauled around behind the boat.

I started off with a nearly new "budget" dinghy. It had a slatted floor, made from fairly thin wooden slats held together by webbing, a wooden transom with an aluminium plate on it to take the outboard clamps, and an aluminium seat. The oars were alloy tubes with plastic blades and they attached to the boat via folding pins instead of rowlocks. All pretty much standard these days on that level of dinghy.

After about six months the floor slats began to crack, so I made up three bigger floor boards from 10 mm marine ply, which I coated liberally with epoxy, paying careful attention to the edges. I then gave them several coats of white paint. They were much stronger, made the boat look better, and because they were close fitting and covered two thirds of the bottom area, they stiffened up the bottom of the dinghy considerably. Six years later they are still in use.

The aluminium transom plate was next to succumb to the effects of sunlight and salt water, and rotted quietly in place. I removed it, and made a doubling piece from another bit of marine ply, which I screwed into place where the plate had been. Again, lots of epoxy and paint. It never rotted.

The forward section valve began to leak, and there was an interchange of pressure between the after section and the forward one, so the whole dinghy began to lose pressure. It became known as Mr. Floppy because it wouldn't stay up. When I got to New Zealand I had the valves replaced and whilst that cured the problem, the name stuck.

The spindly tubular oars were the next to go. I had very tough neoprene rowlocks fitted, and bought a pair of pine oars. This transformed the dinghy. Mr Floppy, fully inflated to the point of being rock hard, with his stiffened floor, became a pleasure to row. I used to scoot up and down the river in Whangarei just for the exercise.

The main fabric of the dinghy never let me down. It has survived sunlight and all sorts of physical abuse and after seven hard years of use, my budget dinghy, improved here and there, is still in use.

Good old Mr Floppy!

6. THE RIG.

Nearly all the boats I met with on my way around the world suffered rig problems of one form or another as a result of the constant cyclical loads placed on their rigs over months and years of ocean passages. Most cruising boats are adapted standard designs, and the rigs and the associated fittings on many modern production boats are simply not designed to withstand the repeated forces they experience on long ocean passages.

This was particularly true of boats arriving in South Africa after their passages across the Indian Ocean, probably the toughest bit of sailing any of us had had to cope with since leaving Europe. The problem with this piece of water is that boats experience two wave and swell systems at the same time, one driven by the South East trades, and the other moving up from the South West as a result of weather systems moving to the East across the Southern Indian Ocean.The South East trades are strong and predominate, but the secondary systems can set up a very awkward and rough cross sea which makes it very hard for the boat to get into any sort of rhythm. As the boat surges ahead, and moves down the face of the wave gathering speed, the apparent forces on the rig reduce with the increase in speed, and she will typically roll, then slow in the trough. Along comes the next crest, the boat lifts on the crest, straightens up and rolls back to weather increasing the load on the rig again. Often the movement and the change of stress are far from rhythmic and the overall effect is to continually stress and de-stress the rig.

Add to this the fact, that, unless they have started in New Zealand or Australia, many of the boats setting off on this passage have probably already covered between twenty and thirty thousand miles of ocean sailing, so their rigs may be pretty tired. You can appreciate why the riggers in South Africa were kept busy. Beyond, with her single spreader rig, has only one set of lower shrouds, and by the time I reached New Zealand I had changed them three times. In each case, when checking the rig at the end of a passage I noticed one or two broken strands on the shroud at the point at which the wire entered either the top or the bottom fitting, and sometimes at both. I fitted a baby stay, in New Zealand to try and stabilise the mid-section of the mast and that helped a bit, but in Mauritius I had to replace the lowers again, and I changed from 8mm 1x19 to 8mm Dyeform which I believed to be about 30% stronger. I now sail with much more tension on the lowers than I have ever done before and they seem to be lasting. The upper shrouds have never given any trouble.

Many other boats also had problems with their lower shrouds, or with their attachment points at the mast.

It's worth considering the relative benefits of the various types of shroud end fittings. Broadly speaking there are two types. Those which are attached to the wire by putting the end of the wire into the socket, then passing the terminal through a set of hydraulic rollers which squeeze it, gripping the wire inside. Once these are on, you cannot remove them. The security of these fittings depends on the fact that huge pressure is applied, compressing the terminal and squashing the wire inside it to a thickness much smaller than its original diameter. A certain amount of that security depends on the skill of the person operating the press and I have seen examples which are bent, or have been almost butchered by poor application.

With the other types, such as the Stalok, the wire is passed through the top of the fitting then splayed round a cone.

The top section is then tightened down on the cone with a spanner, squeezing and securing the wire. The advantage of this is that you can remove the fitting yourself and with a new cone, re-use it if you have to replace the wire. If I was doing it all again, I would have mechanical type fittings like these and carry a set of spares. Stainless steel wire, of 1x19 construction, can't be hand spliced, and you can't bend it through 180 degrees and clamp it, although I have seen someone try it.

I carried a 20 metre length of 10mm Spectra, without a cover, as a standby, for temporary rig repairs. I never needed it but I lent it to a couple of boats who did and they were very glad to have it.

When Beyond set off from Opua for Fiji in May 2012 we were about fifty miles offshore and reaching along in the dark with two reefs in the main and the number four up, in a big sea, when there was a terrific bang and the toggle on the windward lower shroud failed. I was able to tack fast enough to save the mast, and by sheer luck get back to Opua on the other tack, but it was a struggle. The forestay and backstay bear much less stress than the lowers when the boat is sailing downwind or across the wind.

Take a good look at the toggles. Very often the trouble starts on the underside of the top surface, so of course you can't see it unless you take the toggle off to check.

I now carry a spare set of lowers and replace them at the first sign of trouble.

It is a good idea to check the top and bottom terminals of all the shrouds at the end of every ocean passage. The same goes for the mast attachment points, and the spreader roots. By checking just after arrival, if there's a problem you will find it at the start of your time in port, which is better than checking before departure, when, if you find a problem, you will face a delay.

Beyond has a three quarters rig with a very strong keel stepped mast section, which tapers above the point of attachment of the forestay. She has one set of swept back spreaders, one set of lowers, which go to the spreader root and one set of uppers, which join the mast at the point of attachment of the forestay.

Before I set off I added an inner forestay on which I set the staysail and when necessary the storm jib. The inner forestay is set up on a quick release lever about a foot back from the forestay. The backstay is adjustable via a tackle.

There is one set of runners. Some would consider runners to be a nuisance, but on an ocean passage when you very rarely tack, and probably only gybe once a week, they are no problem. In any event, they are solely to add a bit of tension to the forestay and prevent it sagging upwind. The mast will stand perfectly well without them. Many ocean cruising boats have runners fitted this way.

In big winds, with two reefs in the main, the head of the sail comes below the point at which the runners join the mast, so both runners can be tensioned up and kept on, without hindering free movement of the boom.

There is a dedicated track on the mast for the trysail, which I have never used.

Even in the worst of weather, sailing in big seas, I never had the least worry about the rig.

When I left the Clyde in 2010, my plan was to take part in the Round Britain and Ireland Race, then set off on the long cruise. Before I set off I took the mast out of the boat. The rigger, who was also the local dealer for the make of mast I had, went over every inch of it and its rigging. We changed a few fittings and added the inner forestay. Setting off, at least I knew that everything was as good as it could be. One less thing to worry about and worth the fairly modest cost, if only for the peace of mind it gave me when the going got rough.

I had a professional rigger carry out a rig check once a year whilst I was on my way around and I replaced all the standing rigging in the Caribbean on my way home.

7. SHEETS, HALYARDS AND SO ON.

(RUNNING RIGGING).

THE BIG PICTURE.

Essentially you can divide the running rigging on the boat into three categories: Sheets, halyards and control lines. On a racing boat all are subject to frequent movement as the boat works its way around the course and changes are continually being made to sail trim, halyard tension and control line positions to gain advantage in terms of speed or angle and as downwind sails are set and then dropped, or headsails changed. The lines tend to be handled more harshly as well, with lots of tension being applied aggressively during tacks and other manoeuvres. On a typical race round the buoys, it would not be unusual for each boat to tack four or five times on each round, which adds up to a possible fifteen tacks in the space of a couple of hours. Most cruising boats on ocean routes tend to sail down wind, and it's perfectly possible to make a two week passage without tacking at all, and only gybing every few days. On Beyond's passage from the Clyde to New Zealand, which lasted fourteen months, I doubt if I tacked more than a dozen times.

Weight is a big consideration on a race boat, and sheet and halyard sizes tend to be kept to the bare minimum. Coil up a set of headsail sheets, a set of spinnaker sheets and a set of guys, then try and lift them over one arm and you will see what I mean. Of course, weight matters on a cruising boat as well, but a bit more consideration can be given to ease of handling, without going for massively over strength and oversize lines.

HALYARDS. WIRE.

It used to be common to see wire being used for halyards, with a rope tail for ease of handling. This was because the rope tail could be taken round the winch and the wire could take much more tension without stretching. But there were problems on a long passage. A wire halyard under tension at the masthead will gradually cause damage to the sheave as the masthead moves fore and aft. Wire bent round a sheave will gradually suffer strand failure at the point of contact, and a wire halyard cannot be easily shortened by a few inches to remove the worn section.

Halyards on furling headsails have to pass through a halyard diverter on the mast to achieve a suitable angle with the foil. There is inevitable movement between the diverter, which is made of bronze, and the wire. Stainless wire, which is harder than bronze, will gradually cut a groove in the inside front face of the diverter, damaging itself in the process. Bad news all round, because you will have to replace the diverter and possibly the wire, which may jam in the groove it has worn for itself.

These problems may be less important on a marina based boat which does relatively few miles in a season, but if you are spending weeks and weeks on passage, they become significant.

The introduction of high tech materials like Spectra and Dyneema which hardly stretch at all, and do not damage sheaves or diverters, has done away with the need for wire and I wouldn't use wire on a cruising boat if I was planning on going any sort of distance.

BRAID ON BRAID.

This type of rope is perfect for sheets and control lines, where ease of handling matters and stretch is not necessarily a concern. It is very easy to work with and fairly economical to replace. It is, however, more liable to stretch under load and so not so good for halyards. An eight ounce Dacron main sail to fit a thirty eight foot boat is a relatively heavy sail, and once it's up, that weight has to be constantly supported by the halyard, before any sailing tension is applied and before any wind force is exerted on the sail. The distance between the head of the sail and the halyard jammer is a long one, so there's plenty of scope for stretching once the halyard is under tension. That distance increases when there's a reef in the sail and the last thing you want when you are going upwind with two reefs in the main is to have the halyard start to stretch, because the sail will start to take on a deeper shape, which you don't want in strong winds, and sailing performance will suffer badly. So don't use braid on braid for a main halyard if you want efficiency.

SPECTRA, DYNEEMA, AND "CRUISING" DYNEEMA.

These light weight, low stretch materials are perfect for halyards, and high load control lines such as the kicker tackle and pole downhaul on a cruising boat.

They are more expensive than braid; full spec hi-tech lines can cost four times as much as braid on braid of the same size, but they are lighter, stronger and will outlast braid.

The main halyard, which is handled most, and will probably be the longest halyard on the boat, needs to be of a size that will allow comfortable handling. I use 12mm Spectra on Beyond. The outer ends of all the halyards on Beyond are secured to their shackles using a blood knot rather than a splice. It's easier to shorten the halyard that way.

Whilst the main halyard will be handled every time the sail goes up and down and during reefing, the halyard on a furling headsail tends to go up and stay up, often for months on end. That means there's much less handling to be done and that you can get away with a thinner halyard. I use 10mm Spectra on Beyond for the genoa halyard, with its jacket doubled where it passes through the diverter. I have never experienced any significant chafe at this point, although the halyard does take on a slightly polished appearance. Using a blood knot again, it's very easy to shorten the halyard by a couple of inches so that a different part sits in contact with the diverter.

The number four headsail and the storm jib are both set hanked on to the inner forestay. They are smaller sails and very easy to hoist by hand. I use a 10mm Spectra halyard for this purpose and it's dedicated to these sails.

A VERY IMPORTANT LINE... OFTEN OVERLOOKED.

One of the worst things that could happen in strong winds is for the genoa furling line to part when the sail is party furled. Suddenly the sail is out to its full area, roaring and flapping, putting a huge strain on the foil and the rig. If the sail shreds, as it might well do if the sheet stays slack, you are in real trouble and if you can't furl it the only choice is to try and get it down. That would be both difficult and dangerous. At the very least you will have to bear right away to try and sort things out.

If you tie a knot in the line, it won't run through the blocks, and it would be very dangerous indeed to put your fingers into the drum to try and attach, then wind on a new line.

So, to avoid the nightmare scenario I have just described, use a high tech line, and change it often. I changed mine once a year, for peace of mind.

THE ENEMY.

Sunlight and salt are the biggest enemies of sheets and halyards.

When I got to Darwin after a couple of weeks of very hot and spray soaked sailing from Vanuatu, the main and jib sheets on Beyond were so salty and sun baked that I could make them stand up on their own, like the Indian Rope Trick.

The best way to allow them to recover is to hose them down with fresh water, making sure the water penetrates the outer jacket, then let them soak for a couple of days in a bucket of fresh water with fabric conditioner in it. If you are going to be alongside for a few days, and know you won't be needing the headsails, it's a good idea to take the sheets off, and coil them up in the shade.

THE SILENT BOAT.

There is nothing so annoying as the sound of a halyard slapping against the mast, but it can be fairly tough to get them tight enough to stop all movement. I have two positions for my halyards. When I am sailing, the spare halyards are hooked on to webbing loops permanently attached to the collar at the base of the mast, then winched tight and held away from the mast with sail ties passed around the shroud. A very common arrangement. When in port, I make the halyards fast to webbing straps permanently attached to the toe rail, which keeps them well clear of the mast. The use of webbing does away with metal to metal contact which would occur if the snap shackles on the halyards were made fast directly to the aluminium rail or the stainless eyes at the foot of the mast. This arrangement provides a little "give" and makes it easier to haul the halyard really tight. If you don't have webbing, just strip the cover from an old sheet, melt the ends and pass it through the hole in the toe rail, sewing the ends together to form a loop.

In light weather at sea, when there is a swell running, the boom will almost constantly move as the pressure on the sail builds and then eases. Down aft, the mainsheet blocks are attached to the eyes on the boom with Dyneema loops and the clew of the main is held down on to the boom with a Dyneema strop, with the outhaul lashed on to the clew ring. In this way, I have done away with the shackles which would otherwise clink and rattle as the boom moved. In general, I have used soft attachments wherever possible on the boat in an effort to promote silent sailing.

POSTSCRIPT: DOCKING LINES.

Docking lines are quite different from all the other lines we have been talking about, because you want them to stretch. This is because we want the load to come on to the cleats gently as the boat moves around a bit on its berth. For that reason they are usually three strand laid up, or braided with a forgiving inner core. Don't use old halyards or sheets for docking lines, because they don't stretch much and as the boat moves around the load will come onto the cleats more suddenly, with the weight of the boat "snatching" at the points where the lines are made fast. This repetitive shock load will eventually destroy the seal between the cleat or toe rail and the deck beneath it, and a leak will develop.

8. SAIL HANDLING.

ROUTINES FOR SINGLE HANDERS.

Having sailed as far as I have on Beyond, I have some very fixed routines for sail handling, developed over many repetitions during days and nights of passage making, in fair weather and foul. I have found that if I stick to them and do things in a set order I am more likely to achieve a safe and successful outcome and less likely to find things escalating into a downward spiral of chaos and possible damage. All of the routines I describe below are for single handed work, but they work just as well with two. If I occasionally seem to be stating the obvious, I apologise!

Of course, the routines I have settled on may not be the very best way of doing the things they apply to, and they may need some tweaking to work successfully on a different boat with a different layout, but they work for me, on my particular boat, when I am on my own. Such routines continue to evolve, but the longer you go on using them the smaller the changes will become. There is always the chance that someone with a fresh pair of eyes will come on board in the future and suggest a change. If they do, I will certainly listen.

Before we go on to talk about more specific sail handling issues, it is worth looking at a few general rules about handling the lines which control the sails. If you follow them you will have a much better chance of handling your sails successfully, without hurting yourself.

ROPES HAVE MEMORIES.

All ropes have memories. To help a line lie neatly in its coil and, more importantly, to help it to uncoil without a snag or kink, you have to coil it down the same way every time, making the same size of loop.

This may seem a little obvious, but it becomes very important in the dark, when you want to get a sail down quickly or a reef in. On these occasions you need to know which part of the coil to pick up, and which way to lay it flat so that it runs out cleanly. When you are single-handed and you are the only one handling the lines, you and your halyards will get into a routine and you will get along fine. If someone else comes on board, and tries to coil a line down a different way, the rope will object and will probably try and lie in a figure of eight or may even kink.

If you are coiling the free part of a rope like a sheet or halyard, where one end is made fast, possibly at a jammer or on a winch, always start from the fixed end and coil towards the free end. That way there is a better chance that any twists will work their way out, because the free end can rotate.

Sometimes when you are getting ready for a sail change or to lower a sail, it pays to flake the halyard and lay it along the cockpit seat or the deck instead of taking it straight off the coil.

If you do end up with a rope which persistently wants to twist, let the whole thing out over the stern and allow it to trail along behind the boat for five minutes or so as you go along. The rope will rotate, and as it does so the twists will work their way out of it. Bring the rope in gradually, making very precise coils in the right direction, lay the coil flat somewhere to settle, and you will find that the rope settles back into its proper behaviour pattern. If you are dealing with something like a docking line which has two free ends, let it all out and leave it for few minutes, then pull it in, letting the other end out into the boat's wake as you do so. Let that sit for a few minutes then bring it all in and coil as before. It works every time.

After a sail change or a reefing operation you will probably end up with a lot of loose line lying around in the cockpit. Always attend to the housekeeping straight away and restore order before you do anything else. This is doubly important in the dark, in deteriorating weather.

HANDLING LINES.

LETTING GO.

When you go to ease a sheet or halyard that is under strain, always keep the hand gripping the line well back from the winch. Never just throw off the turns when a line is under tension, instead keep some tension on the line, hand well back, take the first couple of turns off and ease the line out around the winch drum. That way there is less chance of the line jumping. If it does, there is less chance of your hand getting involved. You need to keep control of the line, but safely. There is a lot of stored energy in a very highly loaded line, which, if released suddenly, can cause a lot of damage, probably to you.

A clutch is a great device, but it is either on, or off, there is no halfway point. If you need to let go of a halyard that has a lot of tension on it, it may be that this tension prevents you from operating the clutch. In this case, put a turn of the line round a winch and take some tension with the winch handle. Keeping the tension on the line with the winch, open the clutch, and ease the line out. It takes few seconds longer, but you will, of course, have been thinking ahead, won't you, so you will have time in hand.

Even if there is not a great deal of tension on the line, it's always safest to take a turn or half a turn round a winch before you open a clutch to enable you to keep control. Trying to stop a runaway line by gripping it more tightly can cause a bad rope burn, as I discovered as a youngster when I was lowering a spinnaker during a race. The sail filled with a bang and the halyard tried to run out. Being very keen back then, I tried to stop it by hanging on to the halyard and wound up in hospital in a great deal of pain. One problem with gloves is that they trap moisture, and wearing them for long periods softens the skin on your hands, and turns your fingers into a wrinkled mess. After a few months of continuous sailing without gloves your hands will become hard enough so that you do not need them, and I never wear them now, unless it is very cold. An old sailor once told me that the way to toughen your hands was to pee on them. I was never sure whether or not he was serious. I tried it once, but it made such a mess that I gave the idea up.

A LITTLE TIP.

One neat way of controlling the halyard when you are short-handed and want to drop a headsail or a downwind sail like an asymmetric, or a spinnaker, is to pass the coiled halyard under the rail at the stern and let the halyard stream out straight in the water behind the boat. The water creates a surprising amount of drag and you can open the clutch safely and go forward to gather the sail. The more sail you pull down, the less halyard there is in the water, so just when you need less drag on the halyard, you get it. We used this trick often when lowering the spinnaker, when racing, because there is always a tendency for the person on the halyard to worry about the sail running away with them, and possibly going into the water. They play safe and often don't give the folk on deck enough slack.

It's well worth a try, even if there are crew on board, because it frees up one person at a busy time.

STOPPER KNOTS.

If you are going to put a stopper knot at the end of a sheet or halyard to prevent it running through a block or a fairlead, always use a figure of eight knot, which will not jam, rather than an overhand knot, which will.

Put the knot at least a metre back from the end of the line.

The reason for this is that if the line runs out under strain and the knot hits the block, you will have a metre of line to haul on, or put round a winch. If the knot is at the end of the line, you have nothing to grab and it will be like trying to catch the tail of a mouse that has just shot under a gap in the skirting board.

MARK EVERYTHING.

CONTROL LINES.

You should mark all the lines so that you can easily repeat the right settings. This is standard practice on racing boats, but it's very useful on cruising boats as well. The best way of marking a line is to put a whipping on it where you want the mark to be. I make these whippings with a sail needle, passing a few stitches through the line to make sure that the whipping will not come off. You could of course mark the line with an indelible marker but the use of twine has a couple of advantages. Firstly you can feel the mark at night, which can be very useful when you may be looking at the sail or the wind angle screen. Secondly, if you want to move the mark, as you may do at some time, you can just cut the twine off and re-locate the whipping. If your marks are on with marking pen, and you need to change their position by a few inches, you will end up with a confusing array of extra marks. Twine also allows you to use two colours, one colour for one position and one for another.

The real value of the marks comes in the dark when you could be in a situation such as having your head under the spray hood, grinding in a reefing line with your head torch shining on the winch. Get to trust your marks, and you won't have to try and look at the sail and the winch at the same time.

JIB CARS, FURLING LINE AND BACKSTAY.

On Beyond, I have only two positions for the jib cars. One, a metre or so back from the front of the track, which is used when the sail is fully out, and another right forward for when I have a few rolls in the sail. The mark on the car control line for the fully out position is done with green twine, and the mark for the forward position is done with red.

The backstay tackle is similarly marked, green for light to moderate weather, and red for full on, in strong winds.

The genoa furling line is also marked. One sewn on mark, which comes just past the clutch when the sail is fully out and two marks which will be just at the clutch when the sail is furled to the point where I will have the cars at their forward position and the backstay on the hard weather position. The position of these marks has been determined over many hours of sailing, and I know that if I set the car lines and the backstay up on green, or on the red marks, and the furling line on one or two marks, the whole thing will be more or less correct for either moderate, or strong conditions. In the log, I just write, "changed to R" or in easing weather, "changed to G".

All the other control lines, such as the outhaul for the mainsail and the kicker, are similarly marked. I know that if I put the main outhaul on the winch and tighten it until the mark is at the winch, the foot of the sail will be completely flat, also, that if I ease it until the mark is just at the clutch, the foot of the sail will be eased.

On an ocean passage, with a cruising rig, you are not concerned with the finer points of matching foot and luff tension, mast bend and so on. You just need to know that the tension is on, or off and the marks allow you to do this, quickly, even in the dark.

MAIN HALYARD AND REEFING LINES.

The main halyard on Beyond is 12mm white Dyneema. It has a single green whipping which lies midway between the clutch and the winch when the halyard is at the correct tension for the full sail at moderate winds. If the wind increases, I apply more tension until the mark just touches the winch, and if it goes light, or I am sailing downwind in moderate conditions, I ease the halyard back until the mark is almost at the clutch.

There are other marks corresponding to the correct halyard position for each of the three mainsail reefs. One red for the first reef, two for the second and three for the third. To take the second reef, for example, I slack the halyard away until the two marks are at the clutch, at which point there will be just enough slack to slip the reefing ring over the horn, but not so much that it falls off again. I have two rings joined by a webbing strap which passes through the stainless eye on the luff. It's the best way, and makes hooking on really easy. This is crucial when you are taking a reef on your own! Once I have the slack on the reefing line pulled in, I tighten the halyard until the two red marks are just at the winch, which gives me the right halyard tension for the conditions.

The reefing lines are different colours, and each has one stitched whipping, positioned so that it is just at the winch when the reef is in hard and you have sufficient tension on the foot of the sail.

Remember this may not be at exactly the same place each time because the sail may not lie on the boom at exactly the same way each time. However, it will be accurate enough.

I also number each of the luff eyelets, with indelible marker, on each side of the sail. If you go straight to a second reef, you will find you have several folds of sail lying above the gooseneck and it's easy to hook the wrong reefing eye onto the horn. The big numbers will prevent you from making this mistake. There is an anti-chafe patch on Beyond's mainsail, which happens to be just level with the luff eye for the third reef. I have drawn a smiley face on it, to help cheer me up when things are getting bad and the final reef goes in.

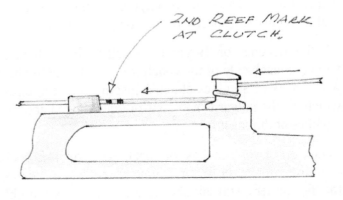

2ND REEF MARK
AT CLUTCH.

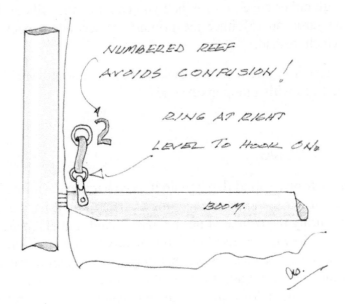

NUMBERED REEF
AVOIDS CONFUSION!

RING AT RIGHT
LEVEL TO HOOK ON.

BOOM.

ROUTINES, PREPARATION, AND EXECUTION.

There are two phases to any sail handling operation, preparation, and execution. Paying attention to the first will help ensure a successful outcome of the second.

All the winches on Beyond are self-tailing. There is a winch on each side of the coach roof level with the hatch, with a bank of Spinlock clutches just in front of it, through which all the halyards and control lines run. There are no winches at the mast.

There are two winches on each side of the cockpit coaming, a primary for the genoa sheets and a secondary for the runners, staysail sheets, etc. If there is a problem with either coach roof winch you can take the tails of the halyards on to either the primary or secondary cockpit winch instead.

I have lazy jacks, but no stack pack. I use normal webbing sail ties with a loop in one end.

FLAPPING.

Allowing a sail to flap will do it more harm and shorten its life faster than almost anything else that might happen to it during the course of normal use. Avoid it at all costs. If you allow the headsail to flap violently with no tension on the sheets the chances are that they will wrap around each other and pull tight. It will be almost impossible to unwrap them without lowering the sail, and you probably won't be able to sheet the sail in anyway.

Even with the sail sheeted in, if the car is in the wrong place and the leech of the sail is allowed to flutter persistently, the stitching in that area will soon give way. Spread out any worn genoa and you will see that the wear is worst at the leech. Flapping is bad! Sails are very expensive. Every time you allow a sail to flap you are throwing away money. Think of pound notes flying off the leech and fluttering away to leeward.

A USEFUL ARRANGEMENT.

An 8 ounce Dacron mainsail on a 38 foot cruising boat is a heavy piece of gear. If the halyard passes round a turning block at the foot of the mast, then through an organiser on the coach-roof then through a closed clutch, just forward of the winch, there is enough extra friction load by the time it reaches the winch to make raising the sail quite a tough job. It is much easier to hoist at the mast, pulling down on the halyard where it exits the mast. To help, I have a V-shaped jammer riveted to the mast about a foot below the halyard exit point and just off to one side of the direct line between the exit point and the turning block at the foot of the mast. I hoist the sail, then stick the halyard into the jammer, allowing the weight of the sail to pull it tightly into the V, which then holds it in position until I can get back to the cockpit, pull in all the slack and take the weight on the winch. I have the same arrangement on the other side of the mast for the staysail, although of course it is much lighter and can be hoisted either from the cockpit, or the mast.

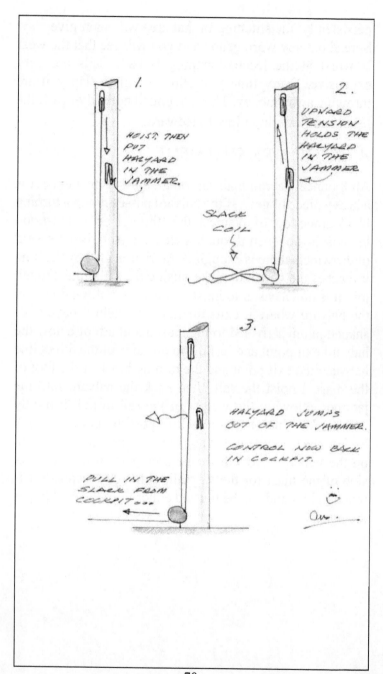

1.

HOIST, THEN PUT HALYARD IN THE JAMMER.

2.

UPWARD TENSION HOLDS THE HALYARD IN THE JAMMER

SLACK COIL

3.

HALYARD JUMPS OUT OF THE JAMMER.

CONTROL NOW BACK IN COCKPIT.

PULL IN THE SLACK FROM COCKPIT...

HOISTING THE MAINSAIL.

PREPARATION.

Kicker off to allow the boom to lift. Main halyard spinlock in front of the winch on. Winch handle ready. Boat either head to wind or fairly close to it, mainsheet eased just enough to keep the load out of the sail, but sufficient to allow the boom end to lift. Main halyard on the sail.

Check that the reefing lines are all sufficiently slack between the boom end and the sail.

EXECUTION.

Leave the cockpit and go forward, removing the sail ties as you go. It's useful to have the tails of the sail ties all lying on the same side of the boom as that on which the halyard exits the mast. If you put the sail ties on properly, with a slip knot, it only takes seconds to free them with one hand as you pass by. That way you can leave the cockpit and move forward along the boom, removing the ties with one hand and holding on with the other, until you reach the mast with the ties in your hand.

Don't put them round your neck. Stuff them down your trousers, or into a pocket.

Haul down on the halyard by hand and hoist the sail at the mast until it's almost fully up, with just the last bit of tension to be applied, then stick the halyard into the jammer, making sure it is pulled tightly into the V. The spare halyard is now lying at the foot of the mast. Don't get it round your feet! If the halyard slips out of the jammer you will be in big trouble and a lot of pain.

Go back to the cockpit and rapidly pull in all the slack. Put the halyard round the winch and hoist the remaining foot or so of halyard until the mark is in the right place. As soon as the winch takes the strain the halyard will jump out of the V jammer at the mast and all the weight will be on the clutch just forward of the winch. Neat.

Kicker on, sheet in, coil the halyard, job done. Get sailing.

LOWERING THE MAINSAIL.

You don't need to be head to wind to drop the mainsail, but it's certainly easiest with the wind forward of the beam.

You may find yourself dropping and stowing the mainsail outside a harbour where there is a sea running. Under these circumstances it is important to keep control of the boom, so you don't want to ease too much mainsheet before you slack down the halyard.

I have a gas strut in the kicker which saves me using a topping lift. This is a great help for a number of reasons. Firstly, it supports the boom without the need for a topping lift. Secondly, it ensures that the mainsail de-powers as soon as the kicker line is eased. Thirdly, it will help lift the boom a little when there is very little wind and you want to sail with some twist in the main.

Because I do not have a stack pack, I use the reefing lines to control the sail as it comes down. The halyard marks are useful here as well. A stacking system would make things easier, but I think they look ugly and I couldn't afford one anyway.

PREPARATION.

Make sure the halyard is on the winch, with the spare properly coiled, clear to run out and the clutch on.

Have the sheet just slack, but make absolutely certain that it is cleated. I often take a half hitch with the tail of the sheet so that even if it jumps out of the jammer on its block, it will still not run out and allow the boom to swing around.

This is very important indeed for the single-hander in any sort of sea, because when you leave the cockpit to put the ties round the sail you will inevitably be on top of the coach roof and probably leaning on the boom with no one in the cockpit. If the sheet were to come free at that point, the boom would start to swing from side to side with you hanging on to it. That's a very dangerous situation indeed, because if you don't let go you will probably end up dangling over the side hanging on as best you can with yards and yards of slippery Dacron flapping about you. So you have to let go of the boom very fast, and you risk getting knocked off your feet by it.

EXECUTION.

Ease the kicker. The boom end will rise and take the power out of the sail.

Ease the halyard down to the first reef mark, pulling in the first reefing line as you go. That will help stop the sail from flopping over to one side of the boom. Ease the halyard to the second reef mark pulling in the second reef and so on. Ease the rest down, make the halyard secure, harden in the sheet and tie it off.

Leave the cockpit, put on a couple of sail ties and return. Do not remove the halyard from the head of the sail. I never do that until I am safely in harbour and I know for sure that I won't need the sail again.

REEFING THE MAIN.

The key to successful reefing is to reef as soon as you think it might become necessary. This allows you to get the job done in moderate weather, when it's much easier, rather than waiting until it's howling, the boat is flying along and there's a lot of strain on everything.

You will need to have the wind forward of the beam, with the boat sailing on her jib, and no weight in the mainsail. If not, you will be fighting the drag created by the wind in the sail and if you are running, fighting the friction between the sail and the spreaders and shrouds as well. That's particularly important if you have swept back spreaders. I have put reefs in with the wind out on the quarter, but it's a struggle, and I usually prefer to dump the main altogether and sail on the jib.

PREPARATION.

Check that the main halyard is on its winch, and that the spare length is coiled and is free to run.

Reefing line on the winch, clutch closed, handle ready.

Over trim the jib.

Check around the boat to make sure you have sufficient room to head up. That's seldom a problem in the open sea!

EXECUTION.

Ease the main sheet until the sail just starts to flap, and then cleat it.

Bring the boat up until the wind is forward of the beam, jib on hard.

Ease the kicker, to let the end of the boom lift a little. If you don't, you will never get the reefing line on hard enough.

Ease the mainsheet until the sail is almost completely de-powered and cleat the sheet. The boat will immediately slow, making life easier all round.

If you are already on the wind, just ease the kicker and the sheet.

Main halyard clutch off, ease the halyard down until the marks are at the clutch. If you can pull in most of the slack in the reefing line with your free hand at the same time you will lessen the chances of it snaking round the end of the boom or of the other reefing lines getting caught under it.

Go to the mast and hook the ring onto the reefing horn. The numbers will help you to get the right one. Don't forget to smile if its reef number three!

Back into the cockpit and winch in the rest of the reefing line until the mark is at the winch, that puts the foot of the sail at the right tension.

Take up the tension on the main halyard until the mark is at the winch.

Sheet in, kicker on.

Back on course.

If it all goes according to plan, I can get a reef in in under a minute. Of course, it doesn't always go to plan, and sometimes one thing goes wrong after another, but if you stick to your routine and get enough practice, you should be okay.

HOISTING AND LOWERING THE STAYSAIL.

HOISTING.

You can hoist the staysail without the boat being head to wind, in fact it's better to do so because this reduces flapping.

When it's not in use I keep the staysail hanked onto the inner forestay, with the halyard on the head of the sail. I have a short length of line made fast to the pulpit with a snap hook on the end of it which I clip onto the halyard just above the head of the sail. This acts as a restraining line and lets me keep the halyard tight without the sail starting to hoist. The sail itself is on deck secured with sail ties. The staysail sheet blocks are on a separate track on the coach roof and the sheets are always left on the sail.

PREPARATION.

Staysail sheets eased with the leeward one on the winch just loose enough to keep most of the load out of the sail but tight enough to avoid flapping as the sail goes up and fills.

Halyard on the winch, spinlock on. Handle ready.

EXECUTION.

Go forward, release the sail ties and the halyard restraining line.

Hoist at the mast, jam the halyard in the V jammer. Return to the cockpit.

Take in all the slack on the halyard, winch in to the correct tension with the halyard mark at its normal position.

Sheet in.

Coil the sheets and halyards.

Because the staysail is relatively small, you can hoist it from the cockpit and I usually do it that way if it's getting rough and I don't want to linger at the mast.

LOWERING.

You want to get the sail down as slickly as possible, keeping it under control to avoid the dreaded flapping and to avoid the slack lower third of the sail going over the side. A good way to do this is to take some tension on the weather sheet so that when you let the halyard go the clew of the sail is held more or less steady.

PREPARATION.

Ease the sheet a little and tension the weather sheet until the clew is just below the centreline of the boat.

Let the halyard go. If the wind is light, or if the staysail is in the lee of the main, it will drop down the stay, almost folding itself as it goes and more or less on the centreline.

If there is still some power in the sail you will have to go forward, sit on the deck and pull it down at the luff.

Put a couple of sail ties on it and attach the halyard restraining line.

Go back to the cockpit and tension the halyard.

I have a length of bungee elastic slightly longer than the foot of the sail stretched along the toe rail from the bow. There is a plastic hook midway along its length, and I slip this under the sail and hook it back over the lower lifeline. It's a quick way of securing the sail without ties, good if you are in a hurry, but not quite as secure as a couple of ties.

SETTING AND FURLING THE GENOA.

When I did the OSTAR (Single-Handed Trans-Atlantic Race) in 2000, I was sailing a 34 foot, three quarter ton design. She had a full hoist, 150% overlap genoa and a relatively small high aspect mainsail. Having the right headsail up was crucial to keeping the boat going fast, particularly in strong winds. I had four different headsails and a storm jib. I did not have a furler so all the headsails and the storm jib were hoisted on hanks. We had strong to gale force headwinds all the way and for thirty days I hoisted and dropped and changed headsails, sometimes as often as five times in the course of 24 hours, in an effort to keep the boat going fast enough to compete, but not so fast that she damaged herself in the big seas that were running. I spent a lot of time on the foredeck, getting wet and hanging on while I got one sail secured and the next one hanked on above it and ready to hoist.

When I arrived in Newport I was exhausted and I had fingers like leather from constantly handling the hanks in wet weather. I persisted without a furler for many more years, but when I started to fit Beyond out for the Round Britain and Ireland race I fitted a Harken furling system and had a headsail made to suit it. The difference was simply life changing. It was like giving a cave man an electric light. I am sure there cannot be many boats on long distance voyages without furlers these days, but if you are thinking about it and your boat doesn't have a furler, get one, and buy the very best you can afford.

SETTING THE GENOA.

The thing to remember is to keep the sail under control. Never allow it to simply power up as it unrolls and crash out into the fully unrolled position. If you do, you will be putting a big shock load on the furling gear, the winch and the bolt rope at the luff of the sail.

PREPARATION.

Furling line coiled, free and ready to run out. Clutch off.

Weather sheet slack, free and ready to run out.

Working sheet with one turn on the winch, winch handle ready.

EXECUTION.

Ease the sail out under control, taking up the slack on the sheet as you do so. I sometimes stop unrolling it with a couple of turns still on the head foil, sheet it in, then release the remaining turns before taking up the final tension on the sheet. That way the strain comes on the foil gradually.

Coil up the spare sheet, do the same with the weather one and drop the coil over the winch.

FURLING THE GENOA.

It's important to achieve a neat and fairly tight roll. To do this you need to keep some sheet tension on as you take up the load on the furling line, but not so much that you impede the furling process. This is easy enough going upwind, when the weight of the wind in the sail will blow it aft anyway, but not so easy going down wind in light weather when there may be very little load on the sheet. Sheet tension is more important under these circumstances because you need to avoid getting a big air bubble trapped in the rolls of the sail.

PREPARATION.

Weather sheet free to run and not likely to drag round anything.

Furling line clutch on.

If there is a lot of wind and a big load on the sail, bear away and let the mainsail blanket the genoa a bit to make it easier to furl.

EXECUTION.

Ease out the sheet and haul in the furling line, keeping just enough slack on the sheet. A good way to keep the sheet and the furling line working together is to start with the hand that's on the sheet about a meter back from the winch. Keep hold of the sheet, and pull a metre of furling line in, allowing the hand holding the sheet to move towards the winch. When your hand gets to the winch, slide it back up the sheet another metre and pull in more furler. The amount you ease the sheet and the amount you pull the furling line will not match exactly, but it will be close enough.

With the sail furled, coil the spare sheet on each side and drop the coils over the winch. There will be a lot of furling line lying loose in the cockpit. Coil that up as well, ready to run out the next time it's used.

You should never have to use a winch to haul in the furling line, if you do, there's something wrong. Check the run of the furling line to make sure there is not excessive friction at any of the blocks. The first and last blocks normally have to turn the line through the sharpest angles. Use blocks with the largest possible sheave diameters in these positions. The smaller the sheave diameter the more additional load will be placed on a line that turns through a sharp angle at that block. Try and arrange the lead of the line in such a way that it does not have to turn through 180 degrees at its aftermost block because this can add as much as 15% to the load, no matter how good the block is.

If you are satisfied that all the blocks are good and that the lead is as fair as it can be, but still having problems, unfurl the sail and ease the halyard an inch or so and try again.

CHANGING HEADSAILS.

Beyond's staysail sets on an inner forestay, which is set up on a quick release lever about a foot behind the headsail foil on the forestay.

It is likely that when you are changing from genoa to staysail, the wind will be building, and when changing from staysail to genoa the wind will be easing. I like to leave the first sail up until the second sail is set, so that the windward sail partially blankets the other one.

GENOA TO STAYSAIL.

I like to leave the genoa up until the staysail is set. Hoist the staysail as already described, setting it inside the genoa and sheet it home. Whilst hoisting, the wind bouncing off the genoa will back-wind the staysail, partially de-powering it and making it very easy to hoist. Once it's up, the staysail will blanket the genoa, which in its turn will be considerably de-powered, making the job of furling it away much easier.

STAYSAIL TO GENOA.

Unroll the genoa in the lee of the staysail. The staysail will keep most of the load out of the genoa enabling you to sheet it in easily. With both sails up, the wind will now be blowing through the slot between the two sails partially back-winding the staysail and decreasing the load on it. You can then lower the staysail as already described, and it will come down very quietly, making it easy to stow. As it comes down the genoa will power up gradually. All very civilised.

A GENERAL PRINCIPLE...THINK AHEAD!

Always, always think ahead. If the wind is getting up, and you think you might want to reef before long, make sure the main halyard is ready, the correct reefing line is coiled and on the reefing winch and the handle is handy. Don't wait until it's time to reef, when things could start to happen very quickly. Even if the weather has been settled for a while, and there's no immediate threat, always have the lines ready for the next likely move. That way, if an unexpected rain squall comes along in the middle of the night, you don't have to go through the preparation phase, all you have to do is have a quick check around and then get on with it, bang in the reef and go back to bed. Always try and stay one jump ahead.

I very rarely shake out a reef if night is coming on, unless the wind is getting really light and looking at the sky it looks as if it's going to stay that way. I would rather wake up in the small hours of the morning with the boat just flopping along, than waken with her flying along under stress and having to put the reef I had optimistically shaken out at dusk, back in again.

Old hands say that if you think it might be time to reef, do so immediately and if you think it might be time to shake out a reef, wait. I could not agree more.

If I am sailing under full mainsail, and am considering a reef, I usually go straight to the second reef.

The thing is, unless it's obviously a short term squall, you won't know how long the wind will carry on building, and it's just not worth messing around with half measures, especially if it's getting dark. In any case, Beyond sails very well with two reefs in the main. With two reefs and the staysail she will cope with just about anything.

9. LOOKING AFTER YOUR SAILS.

SOME CONTRASTS.

On a racing boat, sails need to be light weight and constructed in such a way that they will retain their shape under load. In order to build these qualities into a sail it is necessary to use high tech materials and to construct the sail with far more individual panels than would be found in a cruising sail. This adds to the cost because it takes longer to make the sail and the material used is more expensive to start with.

High-tech material can be less durable than its cruising equivalent, and requires much more careful handling. In general terms, racing sails tend to be much better looked after than everyday cruising sails. At the end of the event they are carefully washed off and stowed in such a way that there is absolutely minimal stress on the material. They are also more difficult for an amateur to repair. As cruising sailors, however, our requirements are different. We do not have to load our sails up to absolute maximum in order to gain a competitive advantage on a windy day, or to come off a starting line flat out and pointing a couple of degrees higher than the next guy. There's a lot of satisfaction in being able to do that, for sure, but that kind of aggressive trimming is simply not required on an ocean cruise.

As cruising sailors we need sails which are durable, which will stand up to rough handling and which we can repair ourselves should it become necessary, because we may be weeks or even months away from anywhere where there is anyone who can do the job for us. Most of our sailing will be done downwind, where the sails will be subject to long periods of moderate loading rather than short periods of more intense use.

CRUISING SAILS.

The material most commonly used for making cruising sails is Dacron, or occasionally a sandwich of Dacron and taffeta, which is slightly heavier. You will sometimes see cruising boats with multi panel layouts, but in general cruising sails are simply constructed, using cross-cut panel layout. Cloth weight will vary slightly with boat size, but in general 8 ounce would be appropriate for a mainsail on a boat of around 12 metres in length.

I have already spoken about the damage that can be inflicted on a sail when it is allowed to flap or flog, or chafe against an object harder than itself, such as a spreader end or a wire shroud.

The other real enemies are bad handling, when stowing the sail, and the effect of UV light which, in the tropics, can be a very serious issue indeed.

HANDLING.

The main and genoa each have one of their edges held taut when they are being stowed, the luff in the case of a furling genoa and the foot in the case of the main, and so it is relatively easy to make a neat job of stowing them. In the case of the mainsail try and use a routine pattern of folds, when you lower the halyard, so that the first fold always goes over the boom the same way and that subsequent folds are made the same size. Pull the sail taut as each fold goes in, let the folds lie in a relaxed fashion and don't overtighten the ties. If you just dump the halyard then try and scrunch the sail up into some sort of order, you are creating dozens of stress lines across the sail. When you put the cover on, make sure there is sufficient air circulating around the sail. Don't cover a damp sail when you are in the tropics or you risk getting mould on it.

When you are reefing the main it is very easy to nip the spare cloth at the leech under the reefing line. Try and avoid that because on an ocean passage the reef might be in for days, and the cloth will quickly wear through. Also, guard against the folds at the luff chafing against the mast or against each other.

When you roll up the genoa, make sure you get a good tight roll, with no big air pockets. If you have to roll the sail away in a hurry, which can happen, and you don't get it right, unroll it again at the first opportunity and make a better job of it.

Some sails, such as extra headsails, will be kept in bags. It is not always possible to fold or even roll a sail carefully before bagging it, and now and again you just have to stuff it into its bag. But if you have to do that, take it back out of the bag and stow it properly at the first opportunity. Trying to flake and fold a headsail neatly on your own is a pain, especially if there is a breeze, but you have to try.

ULTRA VIOLET (UV) DAMAGE.

The effect of UV light on a sail or sprayhood is to fade the material and to weaken it by making it more brittle. At one stage on Beyond the material of my sprayhood became so weak that you could poke your finger through it. UV will rot the stitching as well, and when you try and re-stitch the seam, you may find that the twine just pulls through the fabric. Apart from fading, it is very hard to assess the extent that UV has weakened a sail, but there is one indicator, which is the sound the material makes when you move it against itself, or fold it. A UV affected sail will tend to squeak... so squeaking is a bad sign.

UV will affect other items. I had a favourite T-shirt which became very faded across the shoulders. One evening I went ashore for a shower and took it off. The main part of the shirt came off, but the neck band, which was stronger than the rest, stayed where it was. Old guys may indeed rule, but not for ever.

PROTECTING THE MAINSAIL.

It is impossible to protect the mainsail from UV damage when it is in use. When stowed, the lower sections of the sail will be protected by those which lie on top of them, but the upper sections will continue to lie in the sun. The best thing is to put the mainsail cover on loosely if the main is stowed while on passage. Always cover the sail when in port, whether it is sunny or not.

PROTECTION OF HEADSAILS.

It is usual to have a UV strip along the foot and leech of a headsail and that will protect it when it is rolled away. The UV strip is of lighter cloth than the sail itself, and being at the leech is more subject to physical damage, particularly if the sail is allowed to flap. You need to keep an eye on your UV strip and repair any broken stitching immediately. Stick-on Dacron can be used to hold things together until you can get to a sailmaker. However, even when the headsail is rolled up, there will always be a couple of inches at the top of the luff which will remain unprotected. It is a good idea to lower the headsail every few months and check this as well as the condition of the Dacron at the very top of the boltrope and tape where it first enters the foil. Whilst the sail is down, go up the mast in a bosun's chair, put a soft strop around the foil and slide down it to the deck. On the way down look at each joint and check for any loose screws or sharp edges that might damage the sail. Carry a good few spare screws and a tube of the locking paste that should prevent them from becoming loose.

Loose fastenings are a real problem, because if the foil sections start to move apart or twist at the joints you will not only end up with a damaged sail, the luff may become jammed at one of the joints, preventing you from getting it down. If that happens sew a sail tie loop onto the luff, take a line from it round a block and on to a winch, and try and pull the sail down. Good luck with it.

REPAIRS.

Unless your sails are really weak, possibly as a result of UV damage to their cloth or stitching, or they get into some sort of traumatic contact with a sharp object through mis-handling, it is most unlikely that they will suffer a major tear. The most common problems are localised and arise as a result of chafe, or the failure of small lengths of seam stitching and are easy to deal with on board.

SEAMS AND CHAFING.

As a young seaman I was fortunate enough to be taught how to sew and repair canvas, to do palm and needle whippings, and to splice wire and rope. We loved these skilled jobs and took a pride in being able to do them well. On Beyond I carried a palm, a selection of needles and plenty of waxed twine and enjoyed using them when required. Although in all the time I was away I did not have to do more than a few small repairs to my sails. If you haven't repaired a seam before, it is worth buying one of the many books available which will show you the right way to set about it. The actual work of repair is easy

88

enough and often the hardest bit of repairing a seam is getting enough space to lay the sail flat so that you can get to the bit you need to work on. It is a good idea to clearly mark the spot that requires work while the sail is up, because when you take it down the damage can be infuriatingly difficult to find again.

The easiest repair method for a small hole, or to reinforce chafing points is to use sticky backed Dacron, which you can get from your sailmaker in a roll. Cut the patch to size, wash the damaged area with fresh water, allow it to dry, peel the backing paper off and apply the patch. Very often, if this is a small nick or tear, that repair will be all you ever need.

Repairing a seam or an elongated tear is a little more complicated. Without pre-empting the advice you will glean from your little book on sail repair, the basic thing is to stop the tear or area of broken stitching enlarging itself. To do this, put a few big stitches, of uneven length, in at each end of the tear. These are your stoppers. Then stitch along the material between the two stoppers. Do not worry about making a really neat job. It can be stronger to have the stitches of slightly different sizes. That done, apply broad strips of self-adhesive Dacron to protect the stitching.

I once repaired a headsail whilst it was in use. I was on the East coast of America, approaching Nantucket shoals one night, hard on the wind in light weather, at the end of the solo Trans-Atlantic race. I had a light genoa up, which developed a split where it had been rubbing against the top of one of the stanchions. I could get to both sides of the tear by reaching under the foot of the sail, and with the light wind holding the material taut I stitched the split up in place, then applied two strips of self-adhesive Dacron.

The repair had been done without slowing the boat and I sailed on towards Newport mightily pleased with myself. One of just a few truly satisfying moments during a very tough race.

FINALLY.

Sails are not cheap, or, they shouldn't be. The cost of a sail reflects the standard of the materials used, the care taken in the sail's construction and the quality of the finishing, that is the workmanship and strength of the construction at reef points, tack, clew and head, and so on. It seems to me that there is a sort of three tier structure to the sail-making industry. If you buy from one of the big name, famous lofts, whose focus is racing, or high-end cruising, you will certainly get a good sail, but the price you pay will incorporate a contribution to their research and development programme. That's something you don't need. If you buy from a high volume loft, making cheap sails, usually overseas, you will get a cheap sail, and if it isn't right you could be in difficulty getting it put right. Many of the sails supplied as standard with some new mass-produced cruising boats fall into this category. They don't set well and are unlikely to last more than a couple of seasons.

The middle ground is to buy locally cut and assembled sails. I have been buying sails from the same Clyde-based loft for over twenty years. They have a very loyal following and the owner of the business, himself a very successful racing sailor, takes a personal interest in every sail that comes out of his loft. When I put Beyond's mainsail into a "Big Name" loft in New Zealand for some minor attention, they were very complimentary about the standard to which the sail had been made. I was delighted and so was my sailmaker when I told him about it, but perhaps the most satisfying thing about my sails is that they have retained their strength and performance over thousands of miles of ocean cruising.

Your boat is not just a huge investment. It will become a real friend and you will come to depend on its sails to propel you safely across miles and miles of ocean often in hostile conditions. You wouldn't buy an expensive four-wheel drive vehicle then set off across Africa on a set of cheap tyres. Don't set off on a long cruise with cheap sails, because you won't get far before they begin to let you down.

10. THOUGHTS ON PASSAGE MAKING.

The longer you spend on passage and the further you get from home the stronger the bond between you and the boat will become.

As you leave the land behind and head off across the sea your confidence and self-reliance will build with each passing mile and each passing day. This is particularly true if you are setting off on a long trip for the first time and even more so for a single-hander. Eventually, as you settle into your daily routines, being at sea becomes normal to you, the passing hours marked by the movement of the sun or stars across the sky rather than by repeated reference to the clock.

At night, in fair weather, the emptiness of your surroundings enfolds you like a comfortable blanket. Up in the cockpit, you can lie under the stars and watch the masthead light trace its path across the dark sky, enjoying the presence of the moon and the shadows it casts on deck, listening to little sounds the boat makes, telling you all's well, like the quiet breathing of a sleeping companion. You will become accustomed to the sounds she makes going through the water, to the sound of the wind in her rig and to the sensations you feel through your body as she moves over the waves. Waking from sleep, even in the middle of the night, you will know immediately if all is well, or if she has slowed, or is under pressure. It is a wonderful experience and one that I have enjoyed on countless nights over the years, the memory of which I will treasure when the inevitable creeping constraints of age confine me to the land.

As your experience at sea grows with each successive voyage, you and the boat will grow together, until, even on rough nights, you will feel at home and in control, and that you and your boat are looking after each other.

ROUTINES.

On board, even though you live in a benevolent dictatorship with a population of one, you should have a set of rules to add a structure to your days on board and you need to be tough on yourself about sticking to them. If you are not, you risk letting day to day life slide into a messy shambles.

There is a great satisfaction to be had from lying down to sleep, looking back at the day, running through your little checklist of compliance and knowing that you have not let yourself or the boat down.

Things as simple as always cleaning up the galley last thing before sleep, or cleaning your teeth, are just as important as making sure the masthead light is on, the AIS is running and that anything you might need during the night, like your head torch or your knife are handy. At the end of a difficult day, or on a bad night, when you are under reduced sail, knowing that you have stuck to your routines will go a long way to preventing the nagging uncertainty which can undermine your confidence and spoil your enjoyment of the passage.

My daily routines include writing up the log at noon, calculating the distance to go and working out the likely remaining passage time, receiving the weather grib, sending off emails in the evening and finally cleaning up last thing at night before sleeping.

I also have weekly routines which provide psychological milestones and as such are an important aid to making a long passage pass, particularly if the weather is making things tough. My Saturday jobs include weekly engine checks, working all the seacocks open and closed several times, pouring a couple of buckets of sea water down into the bilge and pumping them out again, thoroughly scrubbing out the toilet area and giving the whole galley area a really deep clean. I can't emphasise the importance of keeping yourself and your surroundings as clean as possible. It's no coincidence that cleanliness routines are amongst the first things new recruits to the services are taught.

There is always something to be done on the boat and I have never ever been bored at sea, or lonely for that matter.

The routine I treasure most of all, is my daily happy hour, which I usually enjoy just as the sun is setting. I sit in the cockpit, and enjoy a couple of beers, think back over the day and think about the remaining days of the voyage that lie ahead.

I carry only beer on board on a sea passage, and I limit my stock to two small cans for each day of the passage, plus four for safe arrival celebrations. If I drink more than my daily ration, there will be less for later on. To make the most of happy hour, you need to be sitting in some sort of comfortable position, relaxed and able to see the sun go down. After a very hot day the first beer goes down quickly; you can almost hear it sizzle. The second has to be sipped. It is a time for quiet reflection and the weather has to be very tough before I do without my evening drink.

PASSAGE PLANNING.

Not many ocean passages are made on the spur of the moment and once underway not many cruisers make it up as they go along, although some do change their plans. There are some very general seasonal rules for making the different stages of, for instance, an Atlantic crossing Westwards from Europe or a passage from Panama to Tonga via the Polynesian Islands. You will probably have read all the books and looked at the passage planning charts and have a fair idea of your planned departure date, months, or even years, ahead of the actual event. In the early planning stages this will be shaped by very general conditions indeed, such as the need to get away before a particular season sets in, or to arrive at your next destination in time for a specific event, such as wanting to be in South Africa for Christmas.

These broader considerations can be narrowed down to take into account the amount of time you want to spend in each country, or the availability of people who may be coming to join you along the way. Cornell's book Ocean Cruising Routes provides invaluable information on the best times to make passages on hundreds of routes and if you stick to the advice given there, and aim for the middle of the recommended period, you will not go far wrong. The book also provides distances that you can use as a guide for passage timing, but you should work out every distance for yourself as part of your planning process. With the general considerations taken care of you can move to the more specific aspects of planning your passage. I never plan, in detail, any further than the next sea passage. I believe that it is bad luck to do so.

When sailing ship companies used to advertise the forthcoming voyages their ships would make, with the dates at which they planned to call at the various ports along the way, the text usually ended with the phrase "God willing and weather permitting", which neatly covered most eventualities.

Old fashioned perhaps, but even today it would be a very foolhardy sailing yacht skipper who would say. "I will leave the Canaries for St Lucia on November the 15th and arrive on December the 9th, or whatever date fitted. On a long passage under sail you cannot take anything for granted.

PAPER CHARTS AND THE PLOTTER.

I was taught to navigate long before electronics had reached their current stage of development. We used a sextant, radio direction finding, and Decca if we were in European coastal waters. Paper charts were used exclusively, and on a tramp ship, which could wind up being sent anywhere, we carried hundreds of them.

Today, the advent of GPS has removed all uncertainty, and combined with a plotter provides immediate graphic/pictorial confirmation of the yacht's position on coastal passages and when sailing in amongst islands (in most parts of the world). But we are discussing ocean passages here and there is still a place for the paper chart, certainly as far as passage planning (and making an ocean passage) are concerned. Because a single ocean chart will cover such a large area, you do not need many of them.

Even on a big plotter screen if you zoom out sufficiently to see your point of departure and your destination landfall, it is very hard to get any sort of appreciation of exactly what lies between. If you do not have a paper chart, your only course of action is to painstakingly creep along the planned track on the plotter, zooming in to a higher level of definition as you go. This makes strategic planning difficult, because you cannot see the big picture and simple reliance on what you see on the screen can create a very unsafe situation if you are not at the right detail level, as the guys on one very well- known round the world race recently found out. So I use paper charts for the 'big picture' aspects of passage planning, and also carry a paper chart for each of the island groups I am likely to sail through on the way, or arrive at. On the final approaches, and once I am sailing amongst the islands, I use the plotter, which you can do with confidence in well surveyed areas such as Europe, New Zealand and French Polynesia, but only with great caution in places like Tonga and Fiji, where you can be anchored in a lagoon surrounded by deep water, whilst the plotter shows your position as being half a mile inland.

One night I arrived in the approaches to Luganville in Vanuatu after dark. I had taken a real beating getting across the Bougainville Strait. I was wet, tired and keen to get anchored. I sailed cautiously up the coast, taking the boat as close inshore as I dared in the pitch black night looking for shallow water. There was no moon and I could only just make out the silhouette of the palms against the skyline. I crept in further, until the plotter showed the boat to be up in the trees... despite the fact that the echo sounder told me I was still in twenty metres of water. I gave up and headed on up the channel, eventually lassoing a semi-submerged mooring buoy, on which I lay until daylight.

STEPPING STONES.

The way I like to get to grips with any long passage is to break it down into manageable portions.

I call it nibbling, breaking the big task down into small bites. It's what enables a pygmy to eat an elephant. When I am planning a straight line passage of even a couple of hundred miles I create waypoints which I think of as stepping stones, such that each successive waypoint is within striking distance of the previous one. On a short passage these might be only forty or fifty miles apart, but they provide handy targets against which you can measure your progress and check the boat's track over the ground. That's particularly important when you are sailing across a variable tide, as you do when crossing the English Channel, when you may have three tides to contend with, one going one way and two the other. If you simply set a way point at your destination and then correct your course every few hours you will end up sailing a lot of extra miles.

To further illustrate the point, imagine sailing across a tide towards a headland ten miles away. If you just keep the bow pointing at the headland you will end up sailing a banana shaped course, and many extra miles.

Suppose you are leaving Mindelo in Cape Verde, for Barbados, which is about 2000 miles away, and you put a waypoint off the North tip of Barbados and head for it, by the time the GPS is telling you that the bearing of the waypoint has changed by even a couple degrees, you will be many miles off your desired track and well into banana-land. So, if you are going to be on a direct rhumb line course and expecting a more or less steady wind direction, such as on this trade wind passage across the Atlantic, the stepping stone approach is even more effective in keeping deviation from the track and extra miles to the minimum.

So it is best to adopt the stepping stone principle and plot a series of waypoints along the track, each about three days run apart, and to steer for each in turn. If you find that you have been set to one side or the other of the track, you can correct and compensate for the next couple of day's runs. It's good to make the distance between the waypoints a multiple of your expected daily mileage, that way you can arrange it so that it's likely that you will hit each target during the day and enjoy thinking about having done so when happy hour rolls along. Of course you can be flexible. As you are approaching one of the stepping stones and are a bit off the track, it will often make sense to head straight for the next one. This approach is less easy to apply on a passage where you have to get through or around a moveable area of calm, such as the doldrums, or the Azores high, or have to avoid depressions passing across your route ahead of you, such as happens on the Southward voyage from Fiji or Tonga to New Zealand. Under those circumstances, you will shape your course on a daily basis depending on the pressure and the wind gribs and you can end up sailing a track which is anything but direct.

As well as the broader seasonal considerations, there may be more immediate short term conditions to take into account when deciding when to leave. Short to medium term forecasting is very accurate nowadays and you might want to go a few days earlier or later than in the long term plan to miss a weather system coming through. There are well established local strategies for some passages. For instance, if you are heading North from New Zealand in April or early May you leave just after a depression has moved East across the North Cape which will give you solid wind from abaft the beam and good speed to get plenty of distance up into the fairer weather. Of course, it doesn't always work out that way, as I describe in the account of my own circumnavigation, 'The Long Way Home'.

With so much information on wind, wave height, swell and so on available, you can of course over analyse and end up waiting forever for perfect conditions. Sometimes it's better to take a balanced view and as long as there is nothing sinister in the offing, just go. You are, after all, an ocean sailor.

A word on waypoints. There are all sorts of lists of waypoints available to aid passage planning. Never, never, head blindly for a waypoint whose co-ordinates you have lifted from some publication or other. Always plot the point for yourself on your chart, or on your plotter screen, before you accept its viability. Always be very cautious when using a listed waypoint in bad visibility, if you are on the coast, or in a crowded area. The chances are that having read the same book several other boats could be headed for exactly the same spot!

DEADLINES.

There is a well-worn cliché amongst cruisers that you should never sail to deadlines, or put yourself under pressure to make a passage out of season just to get somewhere at a certain time. I have already mentioned Cornell's excellent book, Ocean Cruising Routes, and you should follow the guidelines he sets out, aiming to make your passage near the middle of the recommended season. Yachts on the downwind circuit tend to move very much in accordance with the seasons and if you get behind you will probably have to cut short your time at the area you are heading for in order to get back on schedule.

During my time in New Zealand I became friendly with the owners of a classic American schooner called Nina, with whom I was moored in Whangarei. We enjoyed beers together and the owner's son worked on Beyond during her re-fit. With the summer drawing to a close, I was planning to head North to New Caledonia, and they Westward to Australia across the Tasman Sea, a tough enough proposition even in summer. I got away on time and headed North, but Nina's departure was delayed through engine problems and other circumstances beyond their control until they were faced with either postponing the crossing until the following Spring, or setting off at the end of May, well into the Southern autumn. They left Opua at the very end of May and encountered very severe weather, about three hundred miles West of North Island. In a radio conversation with their meteorologist they described being in very heavy seas and having suffered some damage. Further attempts to contact them failed. Repeated searches by the authorities found no trace of the beautiful yacht and her crew of seven. It can only be assumed that they were lost.

ADVICE ON SPECIFIC COUNTRIES AND AREAS.

There is a very useful site called Noonsite, (www.noonsite.com) which is worth visiting. It contains vital information on all the countries normally visited by cruising yachts, and up to date accounts of the experiences of yachts visiting them. These reports do, however, tend to make a rather gloomy read. For some reason cruising sailors seem happier to spread bad news than good and some of us used to refer to it as Doomsite.

GETTING READY TO LEAVE.

With your passage planned and your distances and likely timings worked out you will have a fair idea of what you will need in terms of food, water, fuel, gas and so on, and the process of getting it all on board, which can take days, can begin. I am not a very methodical person and I need to break the tasks down into sectors. One day I will deal with water and diesel, on another with gas, then with cleaning materials, galley stuff and so on, and lastly with food. As the tanks and lockers fill up and the day of departure gets closer, I pay more and more attention to the short and medium term forecast to make sure there is nothing lurking out there to make departure foolhardy. Departure date remains flexible and I usually aim to have everything done with a day to spare anyway. I always try and get away early in the day, and I usually waken with only the dinghy to bring on board and only the last items such as the outboard, the boarding ladder and the oars to stow. The task becomes easier and easier as the voyages go on until you can almost guarantee to get it all done without recourse to any sort of list. When I left the Azores to head for Spain, homeward bound on Beyond, I had already sailed over forty thousand miles in her. The upcoming sea passage, which I expected to take about a week, would have been the subject of plenty of planning a few years previously, but I had a lot more confidence than when I first set out from Europe four years earlier. With the weather looking good and an easy sail in prospect, I just went ashore, bought some bread, a few litres of UHT milk and some meat and set off.

PAUSE FOR THOUGHT.

One last thought on this subject. When I have made all my preparations, stored the boat, planned the passage, said my goodbyes and I am ready to lift the anchor, or slip the buoy, I go down below and sit quietly. I empty my mind of the many boat related matters which will have been occupying it over the preceding days. For a few minutes I think about the family at home, about my friends and about the forthcoming voyage.

Then I feel ready to leave.

ARRIVAL.

There is very little to recommend arriving anywhere in the dark or with night coming on. In the tropics, where there is coral around, it's always best to arrive between ten in the morning and three in the afternoon, because the sun is sufficiently high to show up the different colours in the water.

Apart from anything else, arriving in the morning gives you the whole day to settle in and take care of the various tasks that surround an arrival after days or weeks at sea.

On a short passage, such as an English Channel crossing, from Falmouth to Brittany, or a slightly longer one, such as a crossing of the Bay of Biscay, which involves two nights at sea, you can time your departure so as to arrive at your destination in the middle of the day, but obviously that is not so easy when you are looking at a voyage of a week or longer. Anyway, you would be tempting fate to project the hour of your arrival in such a situation.

As your longer passage progresses, you will start to get a fairly accurate picture of your daily mileage, and will be able to look ahead and have a rough idea of whether you are likely to be arriving in daylight or darkness. Four or five days out, you will be able to firm up your projected arrival time. It is very unlikely that you would be able to speed up, so if it looks like you are going to arrive at night, or at nightfall, the easiest way to plan with any degree of certainty, is to slow down.

On a downwind passage you can do this by changing to a smaller headsail, dropping one headsail if you are under twins, or rolling away some genoa. One of the most satisfying landfalls and happiest arrivals of my whole trip was at the end of 2011 when I had sailed South from Tonga to reach New Zealand. On my final night I stayed well off the coast of the North Island to avoid the shipping and headed in at daybreak. As the sun came up it highlighted the colours on the hills and with just thirty miles or so to go I sailed steadily on and rounded Bream Head in the early afternoon. It was a very emotional moment for me, I had come all the way from Scotland and despite a few adventures along the way I had arrived safely at the other side of the world.

I have one final arrival routine. I used to joke that, on Beyond, the voyage was never over until safe arrival drinks were served. Tied up on the quarantine berth after my arrival in New Zealand I poured myself a cold one and thought about the long journey I had made and the summer months that lay ahead. It was a great moment.

11. WIND VANE STEERING GEAR, AUTO PILOTS AND SO ON.

Like many Corinthian competitors, I was very short of cash when I was preparing my boat, Red Alert, for the 2000 OSTAR. Sacrifices had to be made, and I sold my motorcycle to raise enough cash to buy a wind vane steering gear. I missed the bike, but buying the wind vane was the best thing I could have done. When you are sailing solo, over any sort of distance, whether racing or cruising, you are there to manage the situation, change sails, eat, navigate, think about tactics and communications, mend things and sleep. That's a full time job. The boat has to sail itself.

Short-handed or solo cruising is the same. Erick Hiscock, who sailed round the world, twice, two-handed with his wife Susan back in the fifties, complained again and again of the "tyranny of the helm" and described how he and Susan became exhausted by day after day of alternating watches during which it was necessary to hand steer the boat continuously, sometimes in very rough conditions. You can make most boats sail upwind without anyone on the helm, just by trimming the sails, but it's much harder to get one to do it downwind, unless you use twin poles, or across the wind, especially if you have a modern keel form. Most ocean cruising passages are downwind, or across the wind. Steering the boat is tiring and apart from the fact that it keeps you heading in the right direction, on a long passage it is tedious and very unproductive.

I am assuming you won't be carrying and feeding a crew of six or more, who will happily steer, so you need to arrange for the boat to steer itself.

Broadly speaking, there are two approaches to this. Use an autopilot, or a wind-vane.

AUTOPILOTS.

Autopilots, which are electrical or electrical and hydraulic, comprise two basic elements, sensing and actuating. They use low current electronic circuitry to sense the direction in which the boat is heading, either relative to the wind, or relative to a gyro compass, and to transmit a correcting signal to the device which moves the helm, usually a mechanical or hydraulic arm. But the actuating part, the electric motor, which is either geared direct to the arm or driving a hydraulic pump, uses much higher current than the sensing unit. So, you have low consumption when a correction is not being applied by the motor, but relatively high consumption when it is. You can tune out excess movement to take account of sailing conditions, but rough seas from astern or on the quarter will make the pilot work hard. You need to trim the sails carefully to get the helm as near neutral as possible. Sailing with a headsail only, or reefing the main will often help. If you do not, the motor driving the mechanical gear or the hydraulic pump will be starting and stopping continuously. That's probably okay for a day or two, but not, in my view, for two or three weeks.

One of the most common causes of problems on solo races, particularly amongst the less well financed entries, is the autopilot system, and many competitive boats carry two complete systems. This is not really practical on a cruising boat, because there may not be space, and few cruisers would be able to afford such a back-up system.

Having said that, I know of quite a few long distance cruisers who rely solely on their autopilots and seem quite happy to do so.

On Beyond I have an electric/hydraulic autopilot, with a powerful ram, which I use when I am motoring, because when you are motoring you have a continuous supply of power. I also have a wind vane which I use at all times when I am sailing, because its operation is very simple and it uses no electricity. It's a matter of preference. With a bit of practice you can get the wind vane to steer the boat under power as well, but it takes patience.

The auto pilot on Beyond is a good one, with a sophisticated control system and a very substantial pump and ram. Whatever you do, do not install a small lightweight system, unless you have a small lightweight boat. These are fine for steering in relatively calm conditions, when very little helm has to be applied but will simply burn out if used continuously over many days in anything of a sea.

I derive enormous pleasure from seeing the boat sailing along, being propelled by the wind and steered by the wind-vane, which harnesses the power of the wind for its operation, whilst the solar panels harness the power of the sun to keep the batteries topped up, the fridge running and the beer cold.

Sailing this way I am truly at one with nature.

WIND VANE GEARS.

Wind vanes can be divided into two broad types. Those that steer the boat with an auxiliary rudder, additional to and independent of the yachts own rudder and those that use a servo blade to harness the forces generated by the boats movement through the water and transmit these to the wheel or tiller via lines. The servo moves the wheel, or tiller, which then steers the boat with its own rudder in the usual way. There is a third method, where the wind-vane moves a trim tab on the trailing edge of the boat's own rudder, and you can occasionally see this on boats with a transom hung rudder.

There are a number of makes of each type on the market, such as Aires, Monitor, Hydrovane, Flemming, Sailomat and so on. The owners who have them become very loyal to their particular brand and form a close bond with their gear. I have a Monitor, an American gear, which utilises a servo blade and it is, without question, the single most important and best piece of equipment on the boat. I have sailed thousands of miles using Monitors and on my recent circumnavigation, apart from the need to renew lines, bearings and blocks, remarkably few things went wrong. It is the one thing that enables me to sail long distances single-handed. I prefer the servo blade system because it enables the boat to be steered with its own rudder, the shape of which, and whose distance from the keel were determined by the designer, to ensure efficiency and balance, over a range of conditions. When the designer drew the sail plan and hull, keel and rudder profiles he did not intend that the boat be steered by an appendage bolted on behind the rudder. Non-servo gears tend to be heavier than servo gears, and because the stress of steering the boat is transmitted directly onto the transom and fixing points of the gear, it may be necessary to strengthen the hull at these points when installing the unit. Non-servo gears do have one advantage, in that they can be used to steer the boat if her rudder is disabled and you may want to have this option.

Because the servo blade obtains its power from the movement of the boat through the water, the power it exerts on the wheel or tiller is greater at high speeds and windy rough conditions and less in quiet weather. This means that the response is always in proportion to the situation, just like the hand of an experienced helmsman.

Finally, whereas the servo blade on a Monitor or Aires can be swung up out of the water, the rudder blade on non-servo gears is usually permanently fixed down, which creates drag and which, some owners say, creates lateral resistance when turning the boat at slow speed, as you might have to do when turning into a marina berth.

Whether you decide to go for a servo gear or one using an auxiliary rudder, your wind vane gear will assume a personality of its own and will soon become an indispensable member of the crew

I would never set off on an ocean passage without a wind-vane gear and I think anyone setting off on a long trip should put the installation of one right at the top of their list and examine all the options. These gears are not cheap, but in relation to what they will do for you and the contribution they will make to the enjoyment of the voyage, they are worth every penny.

12. WEATHER.

CURRENTS AND FORECASTING.

The study of weather systems at sea is a complex subject and there are many books about it, written by far more learned people than I. It is certainly worth reading one if you are thinking of setting off.

In this chapter, I will talk about what I believe to be the basic differences between conditions on the open sea, and in coastal waters, and try to give you a very broad outline of what I experienced, and what you might expect, on an East West voyage around the world. We will also look briefly at forecasting.

THE SAFETY OF THE OPEN SEA.

The weather usually changes with much less frequency and with much more warning on the open ocean, particularly in the tropics, than it does in when you are in temperate regions, or when sailing close to a coastal landmass.

In early 2011, I made a passage across the Pacific from the Galapagos Islands to the Marquesas, which took twenty two days. I rarely had to touch the sheets, because the wind hardly varied in direction from one day to the next. About once a week the cloud would start to build, and I would experience a couple of days of windier weather and rougher seas, and slightly higher humidity, but then things would quieten down again. The high grey cumulus clouds would be replaced by lovely white small cumulus that dotted the sky all day and turned a delicate shade of pink as the sun set and I opened my evening beer.

A few months later in French Polynesia I lay for two weeks in a lagoon, inside an atoll. Beyond was made fast by a long head-rope to the legs of an abandoned hut, perched on a coral head. The reef surrounding the lagoon was itself surrounded by the open ocean, so although we were inside, as far as the weather was concerned, we were at sea. Day after day the wind blew strongly, kicking up quite a sea, but lying in the lee of the coral head, I was in quiet water and swung gently from side to side. I was uneasy at first, but the guys ashore assured me that although there would be a few rough days from time to time, the wind would not change direction for at least another two months! I did not stay as long as that, but for the two weeks I was there it blew strongly and steadily from the same direction.

A couple of years later I found myself close to the massive South African landmass, struggling to get down the coast towards the Cape of Good Hope, in winds which would die, shift and then build to gale force with sudden ferocity, creating a very steep and quite dangerous sea. It was very tough going indeed and a perfect illustration of the point, that sailing on the open ocean, where temperature and humidity are fairly stable, is nearly always easier than sailing close to a semi-tropical coast line which heats up by day and cools down rapidly at night, or in a temperate region where you will experience the passage of successive frontal systems.

There is nothing between the East coast of New Zealand and the West Coast of South America except water, so if you are planning a coastal passage from one port on New Zealand's North Island to another, you have to be very careful in strong winds with any East in them. That is because the sea which will have been rolling along unimpeded for thousands of miles finds itself in shallow water and builds up very quickly. When it comes to preparing the boat for such a coastal passage you should treat the trip just as you would one on the open sea, because you will be sailing along a lee shore and your day sail can very quickly become something of a struggle as the seas build and conditions get tougher.

The same situation applies on the windward South East coast of Fiji, with the added problem that you will be sailing along the edge of the massive sea reef that surrounds the islands, and if a real black squall comes along you would be safer to stick it out at sea rather than risk trying to get in through one of the unmarked boat passes that lead into the lagoon.

Weather forecasting in these islands is pretty rudimentary. I was on passage North East along the Fiji Coast from Savu-Savu on one such day when without any warning the sky to weather started to darken and the cloud base began to lower. The wind rose and the sea built up quickly and I looked forward to getting to a pass between two sections of reef that I had used before, and that I was fairly sure of. I took in two reefs and changed to the staysail. Just as I had done that, I picked up a Mayday message from another yacht. Already damaged by contact with coral in one boat pass, they were taking water and had tried to get along the reef and back through another pass into safer water. But they wound up being blown on to the reef and were being pounded by the swell and breaking seas. I turned downwind and got to them after about half an hour to try and help, but even reaching up and down fifty yards off the reef was so dangerous I could do nothing except stay in touch with them on the radio and relay messages to the shore. The two sailors on the stranded yacht eventually managed to get into their life-raft, which was, by a great piece of luck, washed over the reef and into the lagoon undamaged, where they were rescued. Their yacht sadly broke up during the night and they were left with only the clothes in which they stood.

Give me the open sea any day, where there is time to think and room to move.

CONTRASTS. THE ATLANTIC, THE PACIFIC, AND THE OCEANS IN BETWEEN.

The weather in the Atlantic is, in the temperate zones, in general terms, driven by changes in pressure and temperature and the passage of low pressure systems. By applying a few simple rules and observing the changing sequences of clouds, wind direction and pressure, it is pretty straightforward to predict what is likely to happen over the coming twelve or twenty four hours.

As you progress South from Europe, you get into steadier conditions, and whilst the East-West passage across the Atlantic can be rough, most of the sailing will be downwind, with only a few significant changes in pressure.

By the time you get to the Caribbean, your day to day weather will be predominantly North Easterly but with quite marked local variations depending on your position in relation to the islands. Caribbean sailing can be rough at times, with very strong winds between the islands and some fierce squalls. You need to keep an eye open to windward all the time and when you see a big lump of black cloud coming your way, be ready for it. The wind will build rapidly and howl for about twenty minutes, then the rain will start, the wind will die, and you will be left floundering and flopping around in a confused sea until things settle down again and you sail on until the next one comes along. Things usually quieten down at night, but afternoon conditions can be testing.

A CARIBBEAN AFTERNOON.

HERE IT COMES

WET & WILD! 1500
20 MINUTES...

LIGHT & LUMPY
20 MINUTES.

There is some tough sailing to be done between the Caribbean Islands and the Panama Canal, with strong winds and very rough conditions off the North tip of the Venezuelan coast. Friends in Martinique referred to the area as the Cape Horn of the Caribbean and urged me to stay well out to sea. They were right and I had a tough passage until I got close to the coast of Panama.

Once you get through the canal and into the Pacific, and venture to cross it, you will be in the tropics, where temperature and humidity are the driving factors. Unless there is something really unpleasant on the way, the barometer changes very little on a day to day basis, other than to move peacefully through the regular pattern of its diurnal variation. In the Pacific, I keep an eye on the barometer, sure enough, but mainly I watch the clouds. Small white ones are good news and promise settled weather, but if the clouds start to build and achieve some vertical extent, as the sun sucks the moisture up from the sea, and humidity rises, you will be in for a few days of rougher going.

A typical Pacific day begins with the sky lightening and day breaking to show layers of small puffy cumulus clouds. The wind, which will probably have been light during the night hours, unless there have been squalls, begins to pick up as the sun rises and the temperature builds. As the morning progresses the wind remains constant in direction, but increases in force, causing the sea to get up a bit, until by around two in the afternoon the wind reaches its peak for the day, probably around a good force four or five and the boat surges along towards her destination. As the heat of the day draws the moisture upwards from the surface of the sea, the clouds may build, but by late afternoon things begin to quieten down and usually, by happy hour, the air cools as the sun sets and the breeze drops with it. By the time the first stars appear you are probably happy to ease along at a slower pace and get ready to settle down for the night. By looking at the sky now and again through the night hours you will soon see any signs of an approaching squall, because the stars to windward will start to disappear. It is often fun to see how well you can dodge these squalls, and I have even hardened up almost onto a beam reach, or gybed away to get out of the way of one that looked a bit dark and threatening. On other occasions I have watched them for an hour or two, without them coming any closer. It is good sport.

Sailing within the Islands that make up Polynesia is a pleasure, they are mostly within a day's sail of each other, and it is not until you head West over to Rarotonga and the Cook Islands that you will get back into the regular trade wind conditions. The same sort of weather will persist until you are at Tonga, where you come under the influence of a significant landmass once again, and sudden afternoon squalls and quiet evenings are the order of the day.

The passage South from Tonga, or Fiji, to New Zealand provides the next contrast as you head out of the tropics, and start to come under the influence of the low pressure systems that march across the Tasman Sea and pass North of New Zealand's North Cape. It may still not be full summer and you will probably experience the passage of at least one very active depression and cold front, with its torrential rain, rapid changes in temperature, and big wind shifts. Your eyes should be firmly back on the barometer, and you might have to slow the boat down, or alter course to let whatever is coming pass through. Above all, you have to guard against getting pushed over to the West of the North Cape.

Despite its usually wonderful summers, New Zealand lies in a temperate zone and as I mentioned earlier, conditions around the coast can change rapidly. Your day to day planning will involve keeping a very careful eye on the barometer and the local forecast. I spent two summers on that coast. The first was one of the worst anyone there could remember, and the second, one of the best.

Leaving the North Island of New Zealand in early autumn, you can use the passage of these weather systems to your advantage. By setting off just after one has passed through and riding North on the South Westerly winds which should predominate on its Western side, you should enjoy following winds until you are back up in the tropics. That's the theory. In fact, my passage North to Fiji from Opua, during which I got caught between two weather systems, was one of the roughest I experienced in the whole four year trip.

Up in the area around Vanuatu, and voyaging West from there along the coast of New Guinea, towards Australia, you are certainly back in the tropics, but not exactly in the open ocean, so the landmass influences the weather again as you make your way past the coast of New Guinea towards Australia.

As you know, Australia is a massive land mass, and one which heats up during the day and cools at night, making its North East coast one of the windiest in the world. Crossing the Gulf of Carpentaria can be very tough going indeed, because as well as the thermal effect of the land, there are strong currents at play capable of creating very rough conditions. The motion was so violent one night that the cooker on Beyond jumped out of its gimbals and had to be temporarily lashed in place until I got into port a couple of days later. The seas were not particularly big, and nor was the swell, but both of them were steep.

Heading West from Australia, towards Cocos Keeling, out in the Eastern Indian Ocean you first have to make your way along the North Australian coast, a massive area of rock and desert. As the summer progresses an almost static area of high pressure builds up, things stabilise and winds can be very light. Not much change in the barometer here, so it's cloud watching time again. Time to take it easy, and rest, because it is going to get a lot tougher before long.

The Indian Ocean can be a very unpleasant place indeed and the passage from Cocos to Rodriguez is demanding. You are in the open ocean, for sure, in fact you are hundreds of miles from anywhere, but unlike the open Atlantic and Pacific, conditions are far from settled. The wind will be out on the quarter, and it will be strong, but there may be two sea and swell patterns, one from the South East and another from a different angle. The swell is big, and very steep. The motion is violent as you roll and surf your way downwind. You may be sailing in gale force conditions for days and days, flying along under just a headsail, hanging on tight and probably taking a bit of water over the top. But there is nothing you can do about it; you have to keep going downwind, because you are headed for a very small island hundreds of miles away. You want to get there as quickly as possible, but above all you don't want to miss it. You will be cloud and barometer watching on this passage, but mostly keeping the boat going as fast as is safe. I sailed for day after day under just a small staysail making around 170 miles a day and watching the big seas and swell roll up behind. The maximum true wind for the passage was 45 knots and the average about 30. There were a couple of clothes pegs clipped to the upper guard wire just in front of the push pit on the windward side, left over from a wash day in Cocos. In the big gust the pegs would slide and rattle forwards along the wire until they hit the stanchion. I always knew we were in a big one when I saw both pegs on the move. I used to think of the wilder bits being one peg, or two peg gusts.

I wrote a poem about it…

The Indian Ocean has a terrible motion,

It certainly seems to me,

The worst by far that ever I've sailed,

Including the Irish Sea.

There's spray in the air, the waves are all square,

And some come over the top,

Rock roll and sway, it's the same every day,

Wishing to hell it would stop.

Cooking's a chore and never a bore,

Sometimes not easily done,

Spill hot tea down your legs, lose control of your eggs,

It's all just part of the fun.

I know that one day, in some isle, far away,

I will rest where the soft breezes blow,

But till that day does dawn, I must just soldier on,

Only nine hundred miles more to go.

The misty shape of Rodriguez Island was very welcome indeed when it appeared right ahead just before dawn one morning, as was the peace and tranquillity of the harbour lagoon and the company of the other cruisers who had already got there.

Leaving Rodriguez and heading South West, you stay well clear of the Southern tip of Madagascar, because of the sea conditions you might meet there, and as the days go on you gradually work your way out of the tropics and start to come under the influence of the high energy weather systems that come round the Cape of Good Hope. Pay attention to the forecast and watch the barometer like a hawk. This part of the Indian Ocean is renowned for the speed at which the weather can change and for the ferocity of the gales that spring up, although that said, the changes are predictable and nearly always follow a set pattern.

Knowing that one of these systems is coming along, you will see the barometer start to fall. It will fall steadily for quite a long period, and the wind will begin to ease down then almost die as the barometer steadies up. Get set. There is a period of about a couple of hours of near calm, with a rather confused left-over sea. Then, as the barometer starts to quickly rise, the new wind will arrive with a bang, from the opposite direction to which it had been blowing previously. Within fifteen minutes you are in gale force conditions and the sea conditions can be disorganised for a while, until the new wind and sea get established. Watch the barometer because as long as it continues to rise, the gale will persist. Thankfully, these systems go through quickly and within a day or so you will be underway again. Very few yachts crossing the Indian Ocean manage to avoid a gale and all have tales to tell when they arrive on the coast of Africa.

I have already mentioned the conditions that you will experience on the South African coast, and having read this chapter you will understand that many of the factors I have mentioned will combine forces here! A big landmass, with large temperature changes, high headlands, a procession of weather systems and some relatively shallow water, not to mention a coastal current that rips down the coast and brings warm water down into a cooler region. South Africa is, without a doubt, a wonderful country, but its coastal waters and fast changing weather can be demanding, especially for a single-hander.

When I finally rounded the Cape of Good Hope and headed North towards Saint Helena, I felt that I was as good as home. The heat and unpredictable weather of Australian coastal sailing, the violence of the Indian Ocean and the anxious hours watching approaching rain squalls were just a memory. The barometer settled down and could be relied upon. The weather followed the Atlantic rules that I knew so well. Uncertainty vanished, system and order prevailed. I felt that I was out of danger. It was like being on holiday.

SAILING IN CURRENTS.

The advent of electronics has made it simple to see the effect a tide or current is having, by allowing instantaneous comparison between speed through the water and speed over the ground. Knowing the times at which the tide will change we can plan our passages accordingly and play games with the course we steer. It is less easy to do so when we encounter ocean currents, which may be much weaker, or occasionally stronger than they are supposed to be, and may be felt over a wider, or lesser area than they are supposed to cover.

The Gulf Stream is good example. When I was heading West towards Newport in 2000, I was very conscious of the bad effect its East-going stream would have on my speed and I was careful to stay North of its predicted boundary. But the edge of the current was away North of where it should have been and I sailed right into it. One very dark night I was well reefed and tearing through the water at over seven knots in 26 knots of apparent wind, but only making three and half knots of forward progress. The sun rose and I could see clearly that we were in very, very, deep blue water, on which floated small clumps of bright yellow weed. The sea temperature had also gone away up. It would have been a joy to be heading in the other direction, but under the circumstances, fighting the current was heart breaking. For several days I did my best to wriggle out of the trap without going too far North and throwing away distance, and then eventually I broke free.

Not all ocean currents are as visible as the Gulf Stream, with its yellow weed, deep blue water and soaring water temperature; but you will often see signs of a current on the surface. These can be as subtle as small areas of smoother, or rougher water, or groups of small Men O'War, which often drift along on the edges of the steam. Just as sailing against a current is a drag, in every way, sailing in a favourable one is a great experience. You are getting something for nothing, and the bonus of moving on twenty five or thirty miles a day further than the log tells you have sailed is a tonic. The surface of the ocean is always changing and after a while you will be able to read it as easily as you do the sky above it.

FORECASTING.

Just as the advent of the GPS has revolutionised and simplified navigation, the amount of data about the atmosphere that is available from weather satellites and then fed into computer models has done the same for weather forecasting.

The forecasts provided are very accurate. On the coasts of most countries VHF broadcasts every few hours provide updates and warnings of anything unpleasant coming along, although in some areas of the Pacific these may not always be broadcast on time. I set up a system such that I could receive a weather grib data file via the satellite phone which was linked to the laptop.

I could then open the file and display the data in pictorial form, and move the model ahead twelve hours with one click of the mouse. To keep the amount of data, and therefore the time used downloading it, to the minimum, I usually only looked 72 hours ahead, which was plenty of time to plan. The pre-prepared request could be sent in a couple of seconds, and the data downloaded in around ten. It was a very good system indeed, and because the grib data covered a very wide area of ocean surrounding my position, I was able to take fairly broad decisions, something very useful on the passage from the Caribbean to the Azores, when it is essential to know the position and likely movement of the Azores high pressure system.

I had two barometers on board. A traditional aneroid one mounted on the bulkhead, and an electronic one at the chart table. The bulkhead instrument looked good and matched the clock mounted beside it, but that was as far as it went. I relied completely on the very accurate electronic instrument with its clear digital read out and its ability to show not only the pressure but also the rate of change, which is probably the most important thing. I would not undertake any passage of more than a couple of days without such a device. Unless it has a very large dial, and can be mounted somewhere where it is completely free from vibration, the traditional aneroid barometer comes a poor second when it comes to ease of use. I have been on boats where the pressure reading would change by several millibars every time someone pumped out the toilet.

ROUTING CHARTS.

There are monthly routing charts available for all the main oceans, showing average wind speed and direction at numerous points, along with the frequency of gales, calms and fog. The predicted strength and direction of the ocean currents are also shown. These will give you a very general guide as to what to expect, but they are a guide only and the information they provide is based on hundreds of observations made by ships on passage and collated over years and years. The fact is that the climatic patterns on our planet are changing, and are changing more rapidly with each passing decade, so whilst the information you see on a routing chart may well be historically accurate, it is becoming less and less relevant to what is going on today. As a result it is not uncommon to experience winds and currents which are quite different to those that the chart has led you to expect. I have frequently found myself sailing in no current at all, or even in an adverse current when there should have been a favourable one. Certainly, the big players like the Agulhas current that runs down the East coast of Africa, or the Gulf Stream that runs to the North of Bermuda, will still be there, but the less well established seasonal ocean currents may be pretty hard to find, particularly if they are close to the equator. Sometimes you will get lucky, but you can't bet on it.

OCEAN ROUTING SERVICES.

There are several sources of ocean routing information available to you as a cruising sailor. They vary from the very expensive, using lots of computer modelling, to those provided by people in the know, such as retired meteorologists, who do it for fun or for a very modest fee. Two of the latter category, one based in South Africa, and one in New Zealand, are outstanding and very helpful.

There are some passages, such as that between New Zealand and Fiji, or between Rodriguez and South Africa, where it is very useful indeed to keep in touch with such people. Their input, based on years of personal experience of the weather patterns affecting the waters you are sailing in, can be invaluable.

However, I found the more formal, theoretical, highly computerised and expensive services to be very poor value. They will produce a very detailed passage plan based on your theoretical speed, and their modelling and advise you on a suitable time to leave. After that, you have to keep them informed, not only of your speed and position, but of the actual weather conditions you are experiencing. As the days go by, your actual progress become more and more different from that which had been inputted to the plan, and it becomes necessary to re-calculate, at a fee...

Perhaps because I have a fairly good grasp of practical meteorology, I found as the days went on that the advice they were giving was pretty obvious anyway.

By the time you have got as far as heading across the Pacific, you will probably have a similar degree of confidence and if reading this part of the book helps you to achieve that, then it will have served its purpose.

13. SAILING IN HEAVY WEATHER.

If you are going on a long distance cruise, you will aim to leave your country of departure at a time of year at which you will be most likely to experience fair weather and which will enable you to make passages across the oceans in time with the seasons. The great majority of trade wind route passages will be made downwind, and whilst the trades can be very strong at times and can create rough conditions, it is possible to get from Europe, through the Panama Canal and on through the Pacific islands to Tonga or Fiji without experiencing any weather which causes real concern. Doing The Coconut Milk Run as it's known.

The onward passage South to New Zealand, has, however to be approached with some care, as does the later crossing of the Indian Ocean, as I describe in my earlier book, "The Long Way Home".

Inevitably, if you cruise for long periods and sail far enough you will eventually get into bad weather where wind and sea conditions are such that you need to change the boat's course, or alter her speed, or both, to make her comfortable in the prevailing conditions.

Oceans of print have been expended in describing how to get by in bad weather, how to work through a weather system, or take the appropriate action to minimise its effect. It's a huge subject and there are some very good books on it. There isn't any point in trying to paraphrase it all here, because the best course of action will largely depend on the type and size of your boat, the direction to your destination in relation to the wind direction and the strength of the crew. So I will just tell you, in simple terms, how I approached it during my circumnavigation, as a fairly experienced single-handed sailor in his late sixties.

THE GOLDEN RULE.

"One hand for yourself and one for the ship…" It's an old and pretty worn cliché, but it is as true today as it was back in the days of the sailing ships.

No matter how much you know about sailing your boat, no matter how strong, experienced or smart you are, if you get injured, your chances of getting your boat safely through a spell of bad weather are reduced and your enjoyment of the passage can be ruined. On land, a broken finger or a cracked rib is a painful inconvenience. At sea, on your own, it can be a very serious problem indeed, just at the time when the boat needs all the attention you can give her. In bad weather your chances of becoming injured are greatly increased because of the motion of the boat, and you are more likely to get hurt when you are down below than when on deck, because you tend to relax. You need to be able to hold on wherever you are on board, and when moving around, both on deck and down below. When I am moving around I do what I call the Gorilla Swing, and never let go of one handhold until I have a grip on another. On Beyond I added several additional handholds below and up top to allow me to do this. Very few modern production boats are built with sufficient handholds, and some have interiors which are downright impractical at sea, although they seem to appeal to the immaculately clad models in the agent's brochures.

If I have to go up on deck in bad weather I always go up the weather side. The boat is more likely to be heeled to leeward, so if you go up the weather side and you do slip, gravity will move you further towards the middle of the boat. If you are on the leeward side and you slip, gravity will tend to move you outboard towards the side. On one passage home from the USA I was in a gale in mid-Atlantic and had to go up to the mast to replace a shackle on the kicker. I hooked on and sat on the weather side of the coach roof. I became so immersed in trying to get the new shackle in and its pin threaded on that I did not see a very large wave coming. The wave burst over the boat flinging her over on her side. I did a forward roll and came to rest with my legs out under the leeward rail. If I had started that little piece of gymnastics on the leeward side, I would almost certainly have gone over the side and been dragged along by my tether until I drowned. Strangely enough the shackle pin stayed put.

You are particularly vulnerable when coming off the deck into the cockpit, and down from the cockpit to the cabin. I have added fore and aft handrails to the top of my sprayhood on each side to help with movement in and out of the cockpit, and additional handholds on the deck head just inside the hatch so that I can hold on as I come down the companionway.

You need a back strap to lean against when working at the galley, and one to keep you in the seat when at the chart table. These are to prevent you being thrown across the boat. This has happened to me a couple of times, and I experienced a brief period of airborne weightlessness before crashing into something hard with the small of my back.

On deck, even when hooked on, if you feel insecure just kneel or sit down. Your chances of falling are greatly reduced and if you have to move around just slide along on your backside, that's why the bottom and knees of your oilskins are re-inforced. On several occasions I have had to work on the foredeck when the only safe option was to lie on my stomach. Not a particularly heroic pose, but it seemed comfortable enough…until a wave went right up under my jacket then down inside my trousers. It's a hard life at sea, as they used to say.

I have yet to find a sailing shoe, or boot, that really grips the deck, so unless it's really cold, I sail in my bare feet. They have yet to let me down.

AIM FOR COMFORT.

Now that we have taken care of ourselves, let's think about the boat. As far as handling the boat goes, there are a few basic principles, the most important of which, I believe, is to take whatever course of action puts least strain on her. On the open ocean, if you and the boat are comfortable it's unlikely that you will get into any serious trouble. You can get into far more trouble trying to beat round a bad headland against a foul tide with a steep sea than on an ocean passage. On the coast, conditions tend to change much more rapidly than in the open sea. In the situation I describe, you have land to leeward, presenting a threat and limiting your freedom of movement, and a target point round which you must sail with a sufficient safety margin of distance off and possibly a foul tide to take into account. A wind shift or a problem with the boat could put you in real danger.

On the open ocean with no land, shallow water, or tide to worry about you have both time to consider your options, and space in which to carry them out. You also have the opportunity to change your mind if things don't work out. If you do get tired, you can put the boat into a safe attitude in relation to the seas and rest. Having lots of sea room increases your options hugely, and allows you much more time to think, or recover from a mistake.

In ocean sailing it is rarely the wind which causes trouble, apart from the fact that it's the wind which raises the sea in the first place. The problems arise due to the interaction between the boat and the seas and swell. When I raced solo, and got into bad weather, it was always a constant balancing act and compromise between the demands of keeping the boat going fast enough to be in the hunt, and keeping it in one piece, whilst getting sufficient sleep, eating enough and avoiding injury.

SLOW DOWN.

But you will be cruising. You are not racing. You are supposed to be having fun. Your aim is to get to your destination in good shape, with no damage to the boat and not in a state of semi-exhaustion. Speed is not important. Aim for comfort. A boat crashing along and taking big impacts from the seas will eventually damage herself, whereas in the same conditions, the same boat slowed down and sailed a bit freer will probably find her way up and over the waves with relative ease, putting much less strain on herself and on her crew. If you feel the boat fighting the conditions and hurting herself it's time to take action. Take a look at the wheel or tiller. Is the auto-pilot or wind-vane having to apply big movements to control the boat? If you are hand steering, is the helmsman struggling? Is the boat heeling too much? Time to slow down. If you are sailing downwind or across the wind, and the boat is struggling, reef the main, or better still take it down altogether and sail on the headsail alone. The improvement will be immediate. On Beyond my biggest headsail has a 110 percent foot, in other words the clew of the sail comes just past the shrouds when the sail is sheeted in hard. I really don't think it is worth having a full overlap genoa when you are cruising. No matter how well the sail is cut, it will not set particularly well when half rolled away, and it's better to have a sail that spends most of its time fully unrolled, than spending most of its time half rolled away.

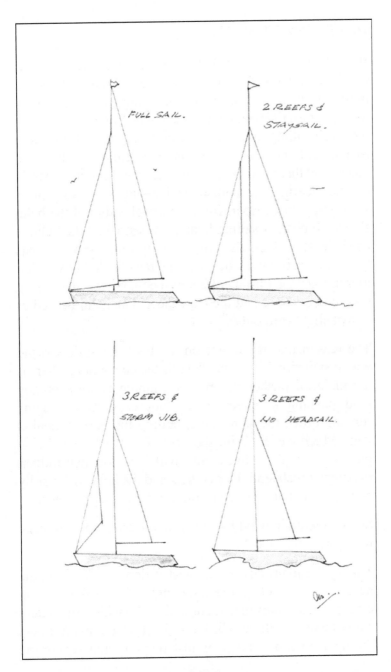

FULL SAIL.

2 REEFS & STAYSAIL.

3 REEFS & STORM JIB.

3 REEFS & NO HEADSAIL.

PULL, DON'T PUSH.

With the wind well out on the quarter or nearly astern, as it's likely to be when you are running down the trades, the pressure on the main, even if it is reefed, is constantly trying to turn the boat up into the wind. You will also have the swell rolling up on the quarter trying to kick the stern round, and there is a constant application of helm to counteract these forces. This has the effect of putting strain on the steering mechanism and results in a swooping, swerving course. Apart from that, application of the helm slows the boat. A sailing boat goes best when the helm is used least, which is why dinghy and sports boats helmsmen sail downwind with the boat heeled to weather to minimise the turning effect of the main, and steer using their body weight and the mainsheet. The helm is used as a final slight trim only.

The reason that it's easier on the boat going downwind with just the jib, is that the jib pulls the boat along, whereas the mainsail pushes it. Imagine running down a bumpy road pushing a wheelbarrow. Not easy. But imagine running down the same road, pulling the barrow behind you? Much easier. With the jib alone, the boat is being pulled down the waves. She will hang on her rudder, making a much straighter course, and the helm will hardly be required at all. An ideal solution for a long passage.

So downwind in windy weather, dump the main and make life easier all round.

Taking the main down is easiest if done early. Trim the headsail in to a close reaching angle. Bring the boat up until the headsail is just about to lift. She will immediately slow down and there will be no load on the main. Sheet the main in a bit until it is just flapping and secure the mainsheet, taking an extra half hitch round the tackle, put the topping lift on, (if you have one) then dump the halyard. Secure the sail and the boom and bear away again. Everything will now be under control, and quieter. There will be much less helm being applied, the boat will be making a better course and consequently probably going just as fast as before. In addition, there will be no need to leave the cockpit again, as you can reduce sail further by just rolling away some jib.

In rough following seas you need to be going at a good speed to allow the boat to stay ahead of the breaking seas, and to keep the apparent wind down. Crossing the Indian Ocean from the Cocos Keeling islands to Rodriguez, I ran before the wind in very rough conditions with just a number four headsail up for twelve days. The boat behaved perfectly, and for many days I averaged around 170 miles a day without even touching the sheets. It was rough, and hanging on and cooking were a problem, but the boat was safe, under very little strain and making good speed towards her destination.

There is a fine line between going at a safe and comfortable speed, and going too fast. At the right speed all will be comfortable, but if things continue to deteriorate, and you find yourself surfing down the faces of the waves, it's time to slow down a bit more. You still need a headsail, probably the storm jib, because sheeted in hard that will help keep the bow downwind and decrease the chances of broaching and getting rolled. Under these circumstances, you can stream lines over the stern to reduce speed, and that will have the additional benefit of keeping her stern on to the wind and sea. Happily I have never found myself in this situation and on a properly planned, in season, trade wind passage across the oceans it's doubtful that you will either.

KEEP SAILING.

There used to be much talk in cruising books about heaving to, and provided you have sea room this is certainly a good tactic to reduce the impact between the boat and the seas, but you must remain in control, and that means maintaining forward momentum through the water and having steerage way. The old idea of lying to a sea anchor was a practice that worked with boats with canoe sterns, but it's dangerous for a number of reasons. Firstly, if you are lying to a sea anchor you are like a half tide rock and you will get battered by every sea that comes along. Like a boxer pinned on the ropes you will just have to soak up the punishment.

Secondly, boats are designed to go forwards, not backwards. That's why they are pointed at the front. Going forwards slowly into the weather is far safer than lying to a sea anchor. If you lie to a drogue or sea anchor you will drift slowly astern, and this puts huge strain on the rudder. If you don't believe me, try motoring slowly astern in flat water, and let go of the wheel or the tiller. What happens? Crash! The helm flies over onto the stops. Try the same thing motoring slowly ahead, and what happens? The boat will slowly wander off course. No drama. No damage.

The tension on the warp of a sea anchor is massive. There will always be chafe, so someone has to go on deck in all the mayhem to move the warp or re-parcel it. That puts that person in danger, and exposes them to the chance of a serious hand injury. You will have no sail up, and therefore no control over the boat and if the warp parts you will lie broadside on to the seas and probably get rolled and lose the rig. Even if that does not happen, you will have a real job to get any sail on.

Of course, you will have lost the sea anchor as well...

Finally, if you stop the boat and lie there, it will take much longer for the weather system to get through, so your unhappy times will last longer. If I had done that on my Indian Ocean passage I would probably have been there for weeks! Keep the boat moving and keep in control. I know plenty of cruising people who carry sea anchors, but I have never met anyone who has used one.

GOING UP WIND, MATCH YOUR SPEED TO THE CONDITIONS.

If your course lies up wind and there's a weather system coming through, you want to get through it and on with the voyage as soon as possible. Under these circumstances, with a falling barometer and rising wind, I always reef the main right down, and keep the boat sailing slowly upwind on whatever tack keeps me clear of the centre of the system and heading out into an area of rising pressure again. I have three reefing points in the main and it's possible to get the main down to such a size that you can sail the boat slowly at about fifty degrees to the wind, without a headsail, taking the seas comfortably on the bow. You need to match your speed to the pitch of the swell and the distance between the crests. Under these circumstances, it's not so much the size of the seas and swell that matter, it's the speed at which they are travelling and the distance between the crests.

It's like driving a car over speed bumps. If the bumps are twenty metres apart with an even gradient between them, you can go along steadily and make good progress, but if they are only three metres apart, look out! Slow down or wreck your suspension!

At sea, you can have a five metre swell coming towards you, but if the crests are fifty metres apart, you will barely notice it. If they are closer together, take care. One way to effectively make the crests easier to handle is to slow the boat. But keep control! You must have steerage way. With a headsail up you will probably go too fast, and create greater impact with the oncoming seas, so get down to the main alone and secure everything on deck. You are now sailing defensively. But sailing defensively like this does not mean sailing passively. You have forward speed through the water, so you have steerage way and therefore you are in control. You will find that having the storm jib up or down, as well as the mainsail, makes a huge difference to forward speed. Keep the jib down, until you are certain that conditions have abated sufficiently for you to really get going, because when you hoist it your speed will increase dramatically, and so will the impact between the boat and the oncoming seas. Even ocean-going merchant ships, which are under constant commercial time pressure, slow down when steaming into big head seas. The owners of these ships would far rather see their ship and cargo arrive a day late than come in with a lot of heavy weather damage. Whether they care as much about the men on board is debatable.

I have a dedicated trysail track fitted to the mast of Beyond, parallel to the main sail track and I carry a trysail, but I have never used it. I think the process of rigging the trysail would be very tough for one person in bad weather.

If you are going slowly upwind and working your way through a weather system, the wind will be shifting. If a front goes through, it may shift very rapidly indeed. The problem is that although the wind may be shifting it will take a while for the sea which it has built up over the preceding days to abate. For a while you will have a situation with the new wind blowing over the old sea, and at a different angle to it. You will therefore have the wind coming from one direction and the waves from another, which can be awkward. As conditions abate and the wind shifts, you may want to tack. Under these circumstances you need to make sure that you tack successfully, because if you get caught head to wind, you will fall back on to the original tack, with practically no speed on, and lie in the trough. In that situation it is tough to get going again and until you do you are very vulnerable.

To avoid this happening, you need to be very definite in your helm movements and careful with your timing. Watch the wave pattern to try and identify the periods where the smaller ones come through. Once you have an idea of a good point in the pattern - probably a couple of waves after the last big one, in which to tack, get ready, ease the sheet a little and bear away to build up speed. You should aim to be turning the boat just as the crest of your chosen wave passes under the middle of the boat because at that point the sea exerts the least resistance to the hull turning. Pick your moment, and go for it! Be bold.

If conditions make tacking a real problem, wait till things quieten down. It's better to stay on a less favourable tack for a few extra hours, and stay safe and comfortable, than risk damage by falling back into the trough with no speed.

In the open ocean, comfort nearly always means safety.

WAVES.

Whilst we are talking about waves, it's worth remembering that the water that makes up an ocean swell or a wave is not moving forward. A wave is an oscillation moving across the body of water. Think of a flag fluttering in a breeze. 'Waves' of material move from the windward edge of the flag to the leeward edge. The flag does not move away from its halyard. If it did, flag makers would all become immensely rich. The water particles that make up the waves in the ocean rotate, with the particles at the top of the wave rotating faster than those at the bottom. The ocean, like the flag, stays in the same place. If it did not and the wind was blowing strongly onshore, most of the water would end up on the land and there would be hardly any left at sea. An odd situation, I am sure you will agree.

The white crests at the top of the great majority of the waves you will encounter in deep water, will nearly always slide down the back of the waves. Deep water crests will only break down the forward face of a wave when the wind is very strong, and the crests become top heavy, or if there is a current or tide running into the wind, undercutting and slowing the bottom portion of the wave and causing the top to tumble forwards. This will also start to happen as the water gets shallower. Of course, there are occasions when a few really big waves will come along with their crests tumbling down their forward faces, but on a properly planned, seasonally suitable passage, the chances of encountering these are, on the whole, slight. There is much talk of "rogue waves" and they do occur, but in fifteen years of going to sea in merchant ships and many winter passages in bad weather, I only ever encountered one. It caused dreadful damage and very nearly sank the ship, even though she was over six hundred feet long. But that was in exceptionally severe weather in mid-winter in the North Atlantic. It was an experience I will never forget and the only time in my seafaring years that I have ever feared for my life.

Where the ocean begins to shallow, if the contour is steep, or where there is a very shallow bank or seamount surrounded by much deeper water, you will almost always experience disturbed water. Try and avoid seamounts altogether, and if you have to cross an area where the ocean shallows, as you often will have to, when making a landfall, or leaving a coast, get across the area as soon as you can. Don't linger if it is blowing. If you are approaching the coast from deeper water, you will cross the hundred metre then the fifty metre contour. It may be that the seabed rises quite sharply at these points, making conditions worse, so don't hang about, get across into the new depth zone and quieter water as soon as possible. The situation will be made worse if the 100 metre and 50 metre lines are close together, indicating a steep decrease in depth. Even if the most direct course lies along or close to and parallel to a depth contour, avoid sailing along it, especially if the wind is blowing onshore, or there is a big swell running in that direction. Get across quickly.

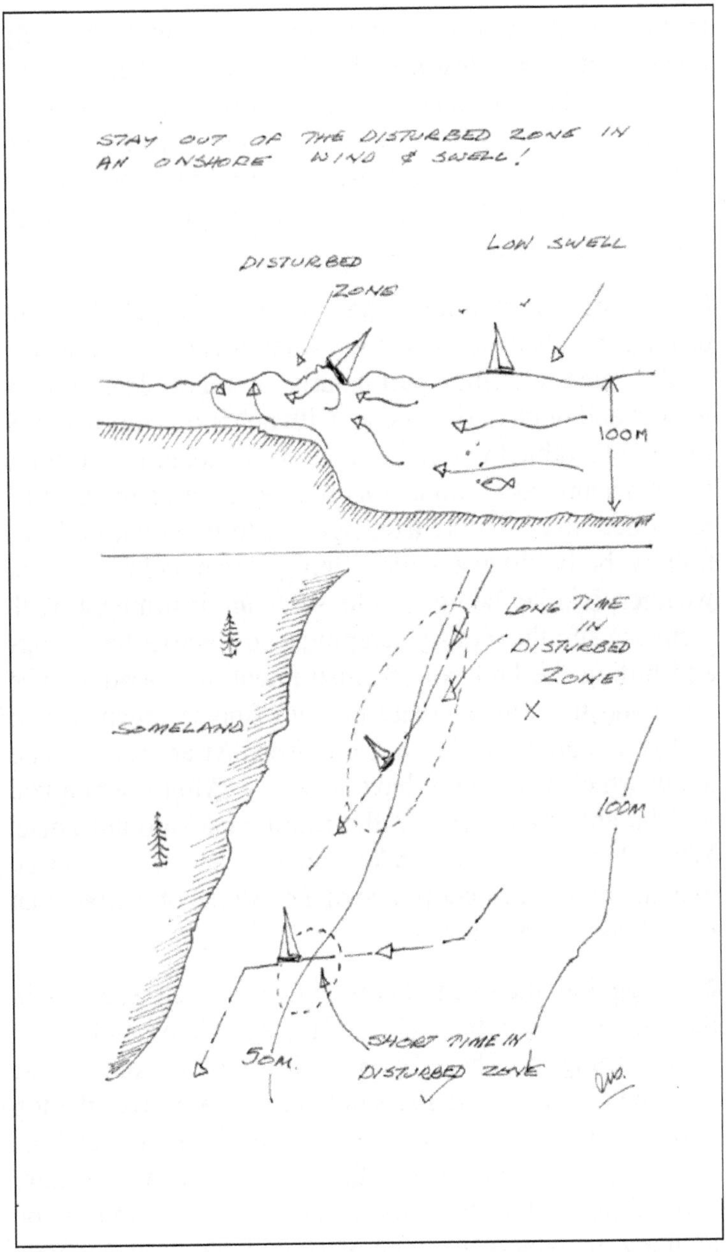

STAY OUT OF THE DISTURBED ZONE IN AN ONSHORE WIND & SWELL!

DISTURBED ZONE

LOW SWELL

100M

LONG TIME IN DISTURBED ZONE

SOMELAND

100M

SHORT TIME IN DISTURBED ZONE

50M

In very shallow water, however, waves will routinely break as they roll towards the shore. That's because the friction of the seabed slows the lower portion of the wave whilst the upper portion keeps moving ahead and with nothing to support it, collapses. That is what, with a big enough ocean swell, creates the breaking pipeline so much appreciated by surfers.

One thing to mention...there's lot of psychology in dealing with bad weather. Very often it is the noise which is the most wearing, particularly at night. If it's very windy, and pitch dark outside, with no moon, you will feel more vulnerable than in the same wind and sea conditions if it's a sunny afternoon. A sailing boat with a mast and a tensioned up rig is like a stringed instrument with a large hollow body, like a cello. Being down below in bad weather is like being inside such an instrument with someone simultaneously scraping a bow across the strings and hitting the body of the instrument with a stick. The wind and the waves create plenty of noise down below, and you soon get to know the noises that are routine and about which you do not have to worry. After a while you will be able to screen out the routine background noise. What should make you take notice is an increase in an existing noise, the occurrence of a new one, or the fact that it's all gone very quiet.

Don't get into the habit of cowering down below. Sit up in the cockpit under the shelter of the sprayhood and watch what's going on. That way you will become more at ease with the conditions. If she's not taking water over the top you can hook on and sit up in on the coach roof for a while. Don't concern yourself with the great mass of white water and rolling swells which may seem to stretch from horizon to horizon. Ninety percent of it will never affect you.

Anything to leeward is history, and anything outwith a fifty yard circle around the boat is unlikely to bother you.

The more time you spend out in the open, facing into the wind and watching what's going on, the more you will become at ease with the conditions and the more you will feel able to cope with them. Stay in control. Don't be a victim.

However, there is something very important to keep in mind. Despite the occasional magazine and newspaper headlines after epic voyages, no one has ever conquered an ocean. The best you can aim for is to arrive at a working compromise with the elements. Don't put yourself in direct conflict with the sea; try and work with it as far as you can. Adapt yourself to its moods. Now and again you may have to be bold, but I believe that ninety five percent of successful heavy weather seamanship relates to caution. The rest is probably down to luck.

One final thought. Each period of bad weather you experience prepares you better for the next and the more experienced you become, the less the weather will worry you.

14. SAILING IN LIGHT WEATHER AND COPING WITH CALMS.

I have always found it satisfying to be able to get the boat to sail in very light weather. In flat water, you can coax the speed up, little by little, so that the boat feeds on her own apparent wind and in doing so points a little higher, creating slightly more apparent wind for herself. On Beyond, going upwind in flat water, or a very low swell, I used the figures 10-40-5 as a guide, because I know that with ten knots of apparent wind at forty degrees on the bow, I can do five knots through the water and that if I am making less than five I need to change something.

Doing this in light weather on the ocean is much harder, because you are rarely in flat water and there is nearly always a swell which will be doing its best to roll the boat around or make her pitch, throwing the wind out of the sails and setting up the infuriating slatting and slamming so familiar to ocean sailors and which can be so damaging to the boat's gear.

As long as you are not in a hurry there is a certain satisfaction in keeping the boat going along in light weather, and if I am able to keep everything steady and the sails are not slamming, or only occasionally doing so, and the wind vane is able to steer, I am quite happy to slide along at four knots, which will get me close to one hundred miles a day. But if I cannot achieve that, and I still have hundreds of miles to go, or if I need to arrive before darkness, I start the engine and run at around 1700 RPM which will get me along at just under five knots and burn very little fuel.

If you decide not to, or are unable to, use the engine and want to persist with sailing, you have to do everything you can to keep the boom absolutely immobile, by keeping the kicker tight, and bracing the boom forwards with the fore-guy, against which you need to tighten the mainsheet.

Under these conditions, soft lashings between the mainsheet blocks and the boom are a blessing, because they do away with the infuriating clinking and rattling that goes on if you use shackles. Under these circumstances, silence is golden.

In some circumstances, in light weather, it is more effective to lower the main and sail with the genoa alone. The boat will be steadier, and the genoa is much more likely to set properly on its own than when trying to do so whilst partially blanketed by the mainsail.

You really need to keep the boat quiet when you are just easing along. I carried a few assorted pieces of sponge rubber which I used to prevent anything in the lockers from rattling, sliding or clinking against whatever was next to it. Small repetitive noises such as these can become massively irritating, can ruin your chances of getting any rest and, over time, will seriously impair your ability to cope with the frustration of making such slow progress.

When the wind drops, the boat slows and the sails will begin to slam more frequently, possibly once every couple of minutes. I can usually live with that, it isn't much more than an irritation, but as it drops further the frequency with which the sails slam will increase to the point where you need to do something. If your course lies downwind, it is worth trying to sail a little higher for a while, increasing the apparent wind and keeping the sails quiet. On a long ocean passage it is far more important to keep the boat moving than to sit almost stopped, even if you are on the right course. The few extra miles you have to cover by sailing twenty degrees above your course for, say, twelve hours, or even a day, are more than compensated for by the increase in speed. Not only that, the fact that you will be covering the ground will increase your chances of getting into a new wind sooner, and that will lift your spirits! When I was racing I often used to think that fast boats make their own luck, and that is certainly true in light weather on a passage race when the faster boats will get into new wind sooner, and start to pull away from the pack, increasing their lead. The same applies to an ocean passage.

But you are cruising, so if there is no way to make progress it's time to revert to your trusty diesel, because there is just no point in letting the boat sit and roll about in the swell. Take the sails down and secure them. If you are in the tropics put the cover loosely on the main to guard against UV damage. Once you have stopped all the rattles and done your best to make conditions on board tolerable, don't just sit there feeling glum.

Try and see the positive side. A calm may be frustrating, but it is not a threat the way heavy weather is. You may well be bored and frustrated but you are unlikely to become injured and it is equally unlikely that anything will break, so try and see the calm as an opportunity.

Think about the last time you were in a real blow and how tired and possibly anxious you were. How much would you have welcomed a day or two of calm then? Try and think of a job that needs doing, or of something that you can do to improve the boat's general condition, or your own. Something which you would not have had the time to do, or been able to do, when you were sailing.

I used to clean the galley stove and the oven, then polish the bottoms of all the pots and the frying pan with steel wool. Jobs such as these help pass the time and, mundane as they may seem, doing them meant that although I may have been going nowhere, I was at least achieving something. It is also a good time to eat and sleep.

Hard as it might be to believe when you are in it, calm weather passes. If it didn't, many of us would still be out there, our sun dried bones rattling around in our cockpits. Watching the first stirrings of a new breeze appear on a flat, rolling, blue ocean is a wonderful experience. You will have been watching the sky and the sea for hours, or possibly days, before things start to happen. To start with, small clouds will form, then dissipate, without any sign of a breeze on the water. However, at least that means that something is actually happening to cause the air to move. Slowly, almost imperceptibly, small darker patches of rippled water will appear, only to vanish again. Gradually, a few more patches will appear, like giant lily pads on a massive pond. You go below, frightened to watch, in case the Gods change their minds and the process stops. You make yourself wait for five or even ten minutes without looking at all. Then, up into the cockpit again, almost frightened to look at the water. But, yes, there are more patches now and you can feel something stirring against your skin. The needle on the wind instrument stops its aimless rotation and steadies up a bit, then flops around again, then steadies... Another few minutes pass, the patches begin to join up. The wind is coming back. You keep quiet, and tip-toe about in case you frighten the new breeze away. Is there really enough to sail with?

There's no point in hoisting the main yet, the boom will just flop about, so you gently unroll the genoa. It almost fills, then fills completely and the boat begins to move ahead, slowly at first, then settles into her stride as the apparent wind builds. The sound of the bow cutting through the water, is music to your ears. Your spirits soar.

Looking to windward you see a solid line of darker water that tells you that the new breeze is really coming. Sitting in the cockpit you trim up the wind vane and relish the moment as the wake streams out astern and you get on your way again.

Life is good.

15. A RIG FOR DOWNWIND SAILING.

GENERAL CONSIDERATIONS.

You already know about my reluctance to fly the main when making long trips downwind and my preference for having the boat pulled along by her headsails. Originally the twin headsail approach developed amongst ocean cruising boats because before the advent of wind-vane steering gear or auto pilots it was the only way that a boat could be made to steer herself downwind. The headsail only approach survives today and makes the job of the self-steering device easier. It's good news all round.

There are a number of options available, some using one pole, some two, some with two sails on the same headfoil, some with one sail set flying, or hanked on to an inner stay and one on a foil and so on. The aim is the same with all of them, to project the right amount of sail area to the wind whilst keeping the rig manageable. It's easy enough to set a towering cloud of sail, but rain squalls can creep up on you quickly at night, and if you are going to get any decent sleep you need to have a rig that you can easily and quickly get down to a manageable size when the breeze gets up. This is where the twin rig has another big advantage. It can be split, one sail up, one down, a bit of one rolled away, and so on. An asymmetric sail or a spinnaker is either up, or down. When I was racing solo, I would fly a spinnaker day and night, because when you race you occasionally have to push your luck if you want to do well. Setting the spinnaker in windy weather is a little like flying a plane. Going up is discretionary. Getting down again is obligatory. In all my solo ocean cruising the spinnaker has never left its bag. Nowadays it doesn't even leave the house.

BEYOND'S RIG.

On Beyond I already had one very substantial spinnaker pole, which was quite tough to handle on my own, especially when the boat was moving about a lot. A spinnaker pole has to be very strong, because when the boat is on a breezy reach the pole comes under both big bending and big compression forces.

When I started to think about my cruising rig, I bought a smaller and lighter pole to use as a whisker pole, which does not come under the same forces, since its only function is to hold the clew of the headsail out to windward. It would have been ideal to have two identical light poles stowed vertically against the mast, but during the months that I was getting the boat ready cash was melting away like snow off a dyke and a second light pole plus the modifications to the mast would have been too costly. So I set off with one long heavy pole and one slightly shorter light one, with an additional sliding ring on the mast so that the heels of both poles could be on the mast at the same time and be moved up and down together.

The boat was already fitted with a furler for the genoa, and in addition she had a removable inner forestay, set up on a quick release lever about a foot back from the furler, on to which I hanked a number four staysail when it got really windy. The inner forestay has its own dedicated halyard. So, I now had two poles, a genoa on a furler and an inner forestay on which I could set a second sail. The number four is, of course, quite a bit smaller than the genoa, so I dug deep and bought a second genoa, cut for running, with hanks, so that I could set either it, or the number four, on the inner stay. It turned out to be an ideal arrangement.

THE SYSTEM EVOLVES.

My first serious downwind trade wind passage was from the Cape Verde Islands to Barbados. I started off sailing downwind with the main and one headsail poled out on the windward side, but after a few days of very gusty weather I decided to see how I got on without the mainsail. The transformation was immediate and everything settled down nicely. I rigged the larger pole on the genoa, to windward, and the whisker pole to leeward on the staysail. That was fine for a while, until I began to realise that I would be better off with the sail which could be furled on the leeward side, and the staysail to weather, so I changed over. Without the main to blanket either sail, both set very well, and when it got very squally indeed, two days out from Barbados, I lowered the staysail and its pole, and sailed on the furled genoa alone, without a pole, which was fine.

Nearly all my Caribbean sailing was on the wind, so it wasn't until I headed South West to the canal that I made more changes to my downwind routine, gave up the two pole system and began sailing with just the light pole on the weather side, and the furling genoa to leeward where it could easily be furled.

I rigged the pole like a spinnaker pole, with its own fore-guy, topping lift and brace, all of which led back to the cockpit giving me complete control over the pole, so that I could raise it, pull it aft or forward, and lower it without leaving the cockpit. Life was getting easier.

The final tweak was to stop putting the jib sheets through the pole end and to lead a running sheet through the pole end instead. If I wanted I could now just ease the running sheet and revert to controlling the headsail on its own sheets as if the pole wasn't there at all. All without leaving the cockpit.

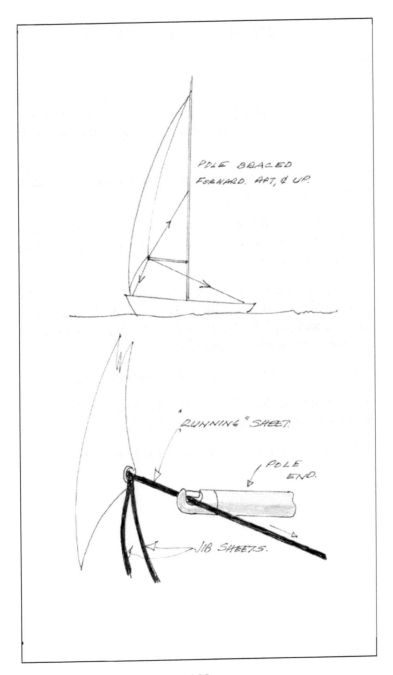

POLE BRACED
FORWARD. AFT, & UP.

"RUNNING" SHEET.

POLE
END.

JIB SHEETS.

NOTES ON RINGING THE CHANGES.

From the top, as bandleaders are apt to say...

Sailing with the full down-wind rig, running genoa hanked on to the inner forestay, poled to weather, furling genoa to leeward, no pole. Easy sailing! Oops, the wind is building...

Drop the running genoa, and hoist the staysail in its place. More wind comes along.

Roll away some furling genoa, until it matches the size of the staysail, it's easy because it's down to leeward... More wind comes along.

Take up the slack on the leeward staysail sheet, ease the running sheet and luff a little. The staysail flops down to leeward and partially blankets the furling genoa, take full control on the leeward staysail sheet. Roll away the genoa.

Drop the pole end to the deck and snug it down.

You are now sailing fast downwind, with the staysail set to leeward, and the pole stowed on deck.

All without leaving the cockpit. Time to put the kettle on.

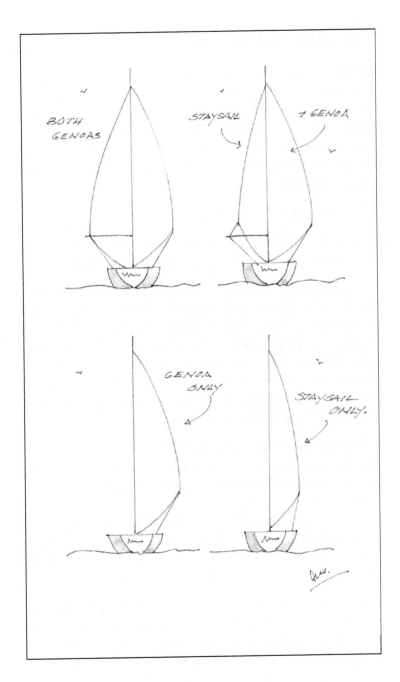

BRACING THE BOOM.

If you are using the main, on a broad reach for instance, or running deep in anything of a sea, it's a good idea to rig a fore-guy from the boom end, to act as a gybe preventer. Most modern cruising boats have swept back spreaders which make it difficult to square the boom right off and under these circumstances the fore-guy becomes even more important.

My system was in two parts:

I had a two metre length of line attached to the boom end, with a soft eye at its outer end. I will call this the short line.

On each side of the boat, I had a purchase with two single blocks, one end of which was permanently shackled to the toe rail just forward of the mast, and the other end of which had a snap shackle which I used to attach it to the short line. The tail of this purchase was led back to a jammer on the cockpit coaming. With the boom eased away, I snapped the purchase on to the short line and heaved it tight, locking it off in the jammer.

Once this was set up I could ease the boom and re-tension the purchase, or ease the purchase and tighten the sheet without leaving the cockpit. To disconnect the fore-guy in preparation for a gybe all that was necessary was to ease the purchase, pull the short line into the cockpit and unsnap the shackle. I could then gybe the boom and attach the purchase on the other side to the short line from the boom end, again, without leaving the cockpit.

When I write about avoiding wear and tear, I mention the importance of immobilising the boom, particularly when reaching or running in a lumpy swell or a sea and moderate or light weather. Even with the kicker and fore-guy on and a relatively tight mainsheet, the boom end will still rise and fall a few inches with each passing wave. To help reduce this to the minimum I put a webbing strop around the boom to which I attach another purchase leading downwards and forwards to a point on the toe rail.

In this way the boom is now held down by the kicker and the toe rail tackle, back by the sheet, forward by the fore-guy and of course upwards by the pressure of the wind in the mainsail.

That should do it.

16. AVOIDING COLLISION

KEEPING A LOOKOUT.

After many years of ocean sailing I have reluctantly come to the conclusion that on the open sea you cannot rely on anyone else to be keeping a lookout. After a number of close-quarters situations with commercial vessels in daylight hours, I am sure that on a couple of occasions there has been no one on the bridge of the other vessel, or if there was, they were immersed in some other task and paying no attention at all to what was going on round about them. I am sure that there are lots of well-run ships on board which the highest standards prevail, but I am also sure that there are many on which they do not.

It seems that now that we are truly in the grip of the electronic age, radar has become the principal means of detecting the presence of one vessel from another, even in clear weather and that if the ARPA alarm does not go off indicating risk of collision, the person on the bridge assumes that there is nothing there. One very windy night on the South African coast I found myself the meat in the sandwich between two ships approaching each other, end on. Each had detected the presence of the other and they chatted on VHF channel six about the alterations they would make to avoid each other. Unfortunately, as they rapidly closed the distance between them it became obvious that neither had seen me despite the fact that it was a clear night and I had all my lights on. There was a big sea running and I didn't want to risk gybing. I eventually made contact and encouraged them to take notice, but until I did they were clearly oblivious to my presence.

Unless you have established radio contact, it is very dangerous to assume that you have been seen.

On another night, a large vessel came up from astern and was shaping up to pass very close to Beyond. I called her and eventually made contact. I was asked for my MMSI number which I gave them. After a minute or two they called up saying they were sorry, but I was not on their register (and therefore presumably not in existence). I suggested that they looked out of the window.

These are extreme examples, both of which occurred in busy coastal waters, but they do illustrate the danger that exists for a yacht on passage. Another thing to remember is that the person on the bridge of the ship probably knows nothing about sailing and the constraints you will be under as far as you altering your course is concerned.

Broadly speaking, there are a couple of ways to decrease the risk. You can do everything possible to make yourself visible and to detect the presence of other vessels electronically and visually and you can do your best to stay clear of the routes they are likely to be following.

TARGET ENHANCERS.

I carry a radar target enhancer, mounted about ten feet above the waterline. When switched on, it responds to any strike from an incoming radar beam, sounding an audible alarm at the chart table and sending out a pulse which shows up on the radar screen of the ship it has detected. The problem with these devices is that if the strike comes in from a ship over the visual horizon, you can come up on deck and see nothing. So you know there is something out there, but you don't know where. Also, there may be more than one ship out there, but there is no way of knowing. Nonetheless these devices are a very valuable aid to detecting other vessels on the open sea, and of making sure that they are aware of you.

AIS.

For me, AIS represents the greatest advance in the avoidance of collision since the advent of radar. I started with a receive only set, which displayed its targets on the plotter screen. I then moved to a transmitting set, with its own screen, showing all the targets and their tracks, which tells me everything I need to know, and provides a great sense of security. I have fitted an external audible alarm which emits a screech that would waken the dead when my guard zone is breached or if there is a converging target which will come within my closest point of approach limits. It is great piece of kit, not cheap, but worth every penny because of its contribution to your safety.

RADAR.

On the open sea, in my Merchant Navy days, when we were keeping watch on the bridge, in clear weather, the radar was never switched on. We used it for collision avoidance in restricted visibility and for coastal navigation when within radar range of the shore, but outwith visual range. But radar has advanced massively and can now analyse the speed and course of other vessels, assess the risk of collision and even propose a course of action. Radar's constant use is universal on commercial vessels and perhaps rightly so.

However, I believe its value on a yacht is limited, and that's not just because I can't afford one.

This is because the plotter provides all the information you need for coastal navigation and the AIS provides detailed information on other vessels and their closest points of approach as well as analysing the risk of collision.

Of course, not all vessels carry transmitting AIS, but the majority do and an AIS consumes much less current than a radar set, and doesn't need a big scanner halfway up the mast, or mounted on a clumsy pod down aft. For me radar is perhaps a 'nice to have item', but one which I did not have and which I never missed.

CROSSING PATHS.

Commercial vessels usually take the course which results in the shortest possible distance between their port of departure and their destination. This means that you will be able to look at your paper ocean chart and mark on it the direct course between, say, The Mona Passage in the Caribbean and Curacao. If you are sailing from the North of the Leeward Islands to Colon at the Panama Canal, you will be able to estimate the period during which you will be most likely to cross the paths of ships on that passage and take the necessary precautions. The Admiralty Ocean Routing Charts show the main routes, including the Great Circle Routes, between the major ports in the areas they cover, and provide a good guide to assist you. On a smaller scale, it's just like making an English Channel crossing. You know the main routes and you know when to expect the main concentrations of ships.

STAY OFF THE MAIN ROAD.

As an example of this technique, draw a line between the inner separation zones at Ushant off the French coast and Cape Finisterre, in Spain, and think of it being the Eastern border of a motorway. If you are heading South, or North, across the Bay, get over about ten or fifteen miles to the East of the line and you will be unlikely to encounter many ships, greatly reducing the chance of a close-quarters situation. The slight extra distance is well worth it.

I did the same when crossing the Pacific, drawing a series of lines between the Canal and the main ports in Polynesia, New Guinea, the Philippines, Japan and so on. I headed for the Marquesas staying well clear of the main routes, and all the way across I saw only one other vessel. There may have been more, but I didn't see them.

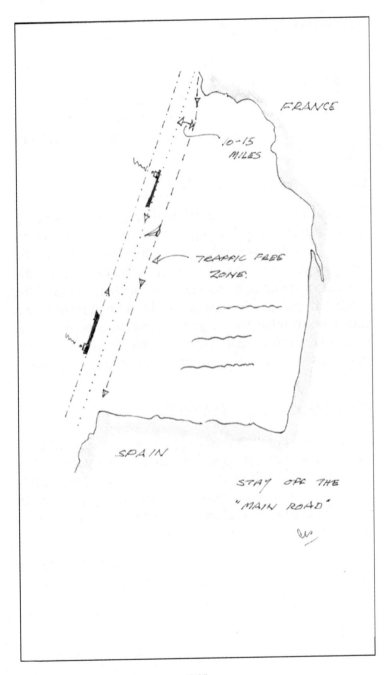

FRANCE

10-15
MILES

TRAFFIC FREE
ZONE.

SPAIN

STAY OFF THE
"MAIN ROAD"

COMMUNICATION.

Don't hesitate to call an approaching ship on the VHF and talk through a developing situation. They may not answer, but if they do you will be able to establish whether or not they have seen you and agree on a course of action. I have enjoyed many a mid-ocean exchange of courtesies this way.

CROSSING SITUATION.

In a crossing situation I occasionally use my hand-bearing compass to check the bearing of the other vessel, but given that both your own boat and compass card will be swinging around a bit, it's easier to check whether the bearing is changing by sitting in the same position in the hatch and marking the other ship's location in relation to a stanchion or other fixed point on your own boat. On the open sea, even crossing ships which should give way, rarely do. Don't get dangerously close just to prove a point!

OVERTAKING SITUATION.

If a ship is overtaking you, and passing clear, try and keep as steady a course as possible and don't hesitate to alter away from her to broaden the angle and build in a safety factor. On an open sea passage I don't like getting closer than a mile to a passing ship and in that situation there is no reason why you should.

If you are overtaking another sailing vessel, the closing speed is likely to be small. It is courtesy to pass to leeward, well off. Don't forget to wave.

END ON SITUATION.

Under most circumstances, particularly when sailing on a broad reach or a run in a big sea, your boat will be veering around probably through ten or fifteen degrees either side of her course. So, if you are closing with another vessel, end on or nearly so, it can be hard for them to tell whether they are seeing your port or your starboard bow, particularly in daylight. In fact they will probably be seeing each bow in turn. Under these circumstances, make a very clear alteration, in plenty of time, probably at least thirty degrees, so as to put your own mind at ease and leave the person on the ship in no doubt.

If things start to look really bad and the wind angle permits it, you can take some of the heat out of the situation by turning on to the same course as the vessel coming towards you. That will temporarily stabilise the situation because you have immediately greatly reduced the closing speed between you and gained some thinking time.

CONVERGING SITUATION. THE ROUND TURN.

If I am in a converging situation with a commercial vessel on a nearly parallel course, I always try to alter course away from her and to do so in plenty of time, so that she is clear about what I am doing. If you are under power, you can just slow down, but if you are sailing that's not so easy, and the best way to get clear may be to take a turn out of your own boat, by altering course away from the ship and sailing in a circle until you are either able to pass round her stern, or are back on the same heading, by which time the relative positions of your boat and the ship will be such that the risk of collision is greatly reduced or removed altogether. You should always try and alter course away from a danger rather than towards it. When you are on a converging course with a ship, you are both sailing in more or less the same direction and the risk of collision increases with each passing minute, but as soon as you turn away from the ship, and you have made half your round turn, you and the ship are heading in opposite directions, and the risk decreases rapidly.

BETTER SAFE THAN RIGHT.

In general terms, you are always safer to alter course away from a danger and to avoid crossing ahead of another vessel. In open water a power driven vessel is supposed to give way to a vessel under sail, but don't bank on it happening. Just get out of the way. There is no point in being run down just to prove a point and anyway you are required to do whatever is necessary to avoid a collision, whether you have the right of way or not. After all, the ship is working, and you are having fun, or you should be.

STAY OUT OF THE DEAD WIND ZONE.

There is another good reason for not getting close to a large ship. Large vessels disturb the wind which blows over them even when they are at anchor. If the ship is going across the wind she will create a dead area to windward and another to leeward. She will also suck the wind in behind her the same way as a big lorry does on a motorway. Stay out of the dead zone or you could find yourself with no wind just when you really need some.

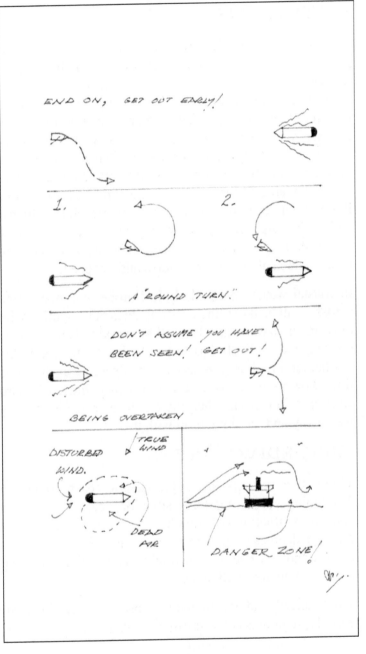

END ON, GET OUT EARLY!

1.   2.

A "ROUND TURN."

DON'T ASSUME YOU HAVE
BEEN SEEN! GET OUT!

BEING OVERTAKEN

DISTURBED WIND.

TRUE WIND

DEAD AIR

DANGER ZONE!

FISHING BOATS.

Fishing boats are a law unto themselves. Other vessels have to give way to them when they are fishing, quite rightly, but it sometimes seems to me that they consider themselves to be fishing from the time they leave port until the time they get back. They certainly have no interest in a yacht. When they are working, they are working and they will be concentrating on what they are doing. At night they may have very bright working deck lights on and probably won't be able to see outwith the circle of their own illumination, even if they cared to look, which is unlikely. Unless they are trawling, when they will be making a fairly steady course at moderate speed, they are also liable to make sudden alterations of course and or speed.

In coastal waters, particularly in Europe, you may come across small boats setting or lifting lines of pots, often with only one man on board. He will be working hard to make a living and probably has to handle his boat, operate the pot hauler and drag pots around the deck, all at the same time. For his own sake, he has to concentrate. It's hard work and dangerous when there is a sea running, so stay well away and let him get on with it.

THE CARDINAL RULE.

When two vessels are approaching each other, a developing close-quarters situation can become a dangerous situation very quickly. As the distance between the two decreases, the options for avoiding each other narrow and risk rises exponentially. The earlier you react, the safer you are likely to be.

Think ahead and try to avoid close-quarters situations entirely, regardless of your rights.

17. ANCHORS AND ANCHORING.

KEEP IT SIMPLE.

Many books on cruising spend a lot of time talking about different anchors and anchoring techniques, and there is plenty to talk about, but it's easy to overcomplicate the subject. If you believe everything you read you will have to carry at least three anchors, lots and lots of ground tackle, anchor buoys, angels, and so on. On top of that you are told that you will need to be competent in carrying out a running moor, a standing moor, and a Bahamian moor.

When I set off I had a thirty pound Bruce anchor with seventy metres of 8mm calibrated chain as my main anchor, and a twenty pound CQR type with twenty metres of chain and fifty metres of warp in reserve. Over the four years during which I cruised, I visited hundreds of anchorages and anchored in coral, sand, mud, stones and various combinations of these. I only dragged three times, each in extremely strong conditions, and my trusty Bruce was all I ever needed.

I lost the CQR in Tonga, and replaced it with a Manson, which I have never used.

Just as in heavy weather you should be aiming to maximise comfort, when anchoring your aim is to achieve peace and quiet and a sound night's sleep!

ONE ANCHOR, PROPERLY SET, IS BEST.

I very rarely lie to two anchors, because I think it's a trap, for a number of reasons.

Firstly, with two anchors down, unless the boat lies constantly in the same direction as she was pointing when you laid them, the anchor cables will cross. But boats swing, twice a day with the tide, and if there is a weather system going through, they will swing to the shifting wind, or possibly lie somewhere between the tide and the wind. You could therefore end up with one, or even multiple crosses in the cables. How would you get out of that, if the boat starts to drag? Only with great difficulty, I can assure you.

Even with no crosses in the cables, if you start to drag, or there's a big wind shift and you want to get out, you will have to raise one anchor first, or slip it. While you are doing that you are losing valuable time and will continue to drag, and when you get the first anchor off the bottom, or nearly so, you will start to drag even faster, and of course you still have to deal with the other anchor. This is a difficult situation to deal with, even in daylight with a good crew. Add a howling wind, lashing rain and darkness and you will quickly begin to wish you had stuck to gardening. For a single-hander this sort of situation presents real danger.

I got caught out in Tonga, lying with a few other yachts behind the arm of a crescent shaped reef at Pangiamotu Island. The weather had been looking unsettled for a couple of days, with an increasing wind, rain showers and grey, building cumulus. Anticipating a blow, I had two anchors down. Around midday a black squall came through. Within the space of a couple of minutes the wind shifted fifty degrees to the left and increased to about forty knots, with driving rain. The force of the wind heeled the boat right over. No longer sheltered by the arm of the reef she began to drag down onto the part of the reef which had previously been on the beam. I went forward to buoy off and slip the warp attached to the second anchor, but thankfully the warp parted, allowing the boat to swing onto the main anchor, which I was able to haul in with the windlass, motoring ahead with the engine to take the weight off the chain. There was so much rain that visibility was almost nil, and so much wind noise that I could not hear the engine. I had no idea where the chain was leading, but I knew I was getting closer to the shore, so I just kept motoring ahead until I saw the white mark on the chain that told me the anchor was off the bottom, and headed back in towards the main harbour at Nukualofa.

I went back to the anchorage a few days later, and snorkelled around the spot where I had been anchored, but I never got the anchor or the warp back. Perhaps someone else got there first.

WORKING WITH THE CHAIN.

On a smaller boat, you can get away with not having a windlass and Beyond did not have one when I first got her. I soon realised that pulling in forty or fifty metres of relatively heavy chain, then lifting a thirty pound anchor in twelve metres of water was not for me, and I worried about injuring my back.

I fitted a 1000 watt windlass, and the gypsy and chain are both calibrated. There is a foot switch beside the windlass which will raise the anchor and a remote switch on a flexible lead in the cockpit, with which you can either raise or lower the anchor. I believe that for single-handed sailing it is essential to have such an arrangement and even with two people it's a big advantage. By the way, don't try operating your windlass without the engine running because you will ruin your batteries. I am sure you know that already, but don't be offended… I have seen it happen.

My chain is marked with white paint every ten metres, and the final stretch before the anchor is painted continuously white, with the mark so positioned that when operating the windlass from the cockpit, you know that when the continuous white links start to appear, you slow the windlass and that when the last white link passes the gypsy the anchor will be just clear of the water. At night, with the foredeck light on, I can see the marks easily from the cockpit. I also know that when letting go it takes twelve seconds for ten metres of chain to go out when I hold down the button, so even if I cannot see the marks I have a good idea of how much chain is out.

You need to be able to slip the cable if you have to, so pay attention to how the end of it is made fast to the boat. Don't shackle it to anything, because if you do end up with all the chain out and the whole weight being taken on that shackle, it's most unlikely that you will be able to undo it. It's much better to tie the last link to a strong point inside the chain locker, with several turns of light line. That way you can attach the buoy and recovery line ahead of the bow, then just cut the line securing the end of the chain, keeping your hands well clear!

One important piece of kit is a snubber, which consists of a few metres of relatively stretchy rope, such as three strand nylon. To one end you attach a purpose made stainless chain hook, of the correct size to match your chain. The other end is left plain. The purpose of the snubber is to take the weight that comes onto the anchor chain.

There are three good reasons for using a snubber:

Firstly, there is no give in an anchor chain, and if the weight is left on the windlass gypsy, the strain on the cable will be transmitted straight onto the drive shaft and then to the structure of the boat. This puts a shear stress on the gypsy drive shaft, which may in time distort or damage it,

174

or its clutch mechanism. Once in place the snubber takes all the load, dampens out some shock loading and reduces the likelihood of the anchor breaking out and dragging.

Secondly, because the snubber is of relatively soft material, it saves wear on the bow roller and reduces the level of any noise transmitted to the inside of the boat from the anchor chain.

Thirdly, the snubber can be turned up round one of the mooring cleats on deck, placing the load of the anchor on the cleat, which is designed to take that sort of load.

Once the anchor is settled in, attach the snubber, make the inner end fast, and then slacken the chain until the snubber is taking all the load. Leave the chain on the gypsy though, even though it is taking no load. If you do not, and the snubber fails or slips off when the chain is slack, your chain will run out and you will lose the lot.

DRAGGING.

In a flat water anchorage, even in a strong breeze, unless the boat is shearing about a lot and trying to sail round her anchor, as some boats do, it is rarely the effect of the wind alone on the boat which causes the anchor to break out from the seabed and drag, because the strain on the chain and anchor tends to be more constant. But if there is a sea running into the anchorage causing the boat to pitch, and you have no snubber, she will snub her chain, causing it to alternately slacken when the bow goes down and then suddenly come very tight again as the bow rises and the chain takes all the weight of the boat. In any situation like this, a steady load is much less likely to cause problems than a repeated shock load, which is more likely to make the anchor break out. Remember, the anchor holds the chain on to the sea bed, but it is the weight of the chain, and the effort required to pull it tight, that secures the boat and helps keep a more or less steady and near horizontal pull on the anchor, encouraging it to dig in deeper and deeper. That is why it is so important to use plenty of chain, and why it is much less effective to use rope, or rope with just a short length of chain between it and the anchor.

If you do start to drag, there is very little point in putting out more chain. If the anchor has lost its grip and moved, the damage is done and the extra weight of another ten metres of chain is not going to make any difference. Besides, the extra length will just put you closer to any obstruction astern such as the shore. If you find yourself on the move, heave up and go somewhere else. It's the only way you will get any peace.

AN ANGEL.

You can help damp out repeated shock load and decrease the chances of dragging even more by attaching a weight to the chain, half way between the bow and the anchor. Any weight will do, but you need to be able to slide it down the chain, and, more importantly, get it back up again, unless you want to be stuck there for a while.

The traditional "Angel" as it's known has a cleverly designed collar, which sits over the chain. Weights are attached below the collar and the whole thing can be easily slid up and down the anchor chain and more importantly, attached and detached. If the boat is snubbing and there's a lot of weight on the chain, you really don't want to spend too much time perched on the bow with your fingers close to the chain. The same goes for dealing with a crossed chain when you have two anchors down. I let my hand get too close to the bow roller when I was anchoring in an isolated atoll in Polynesia and sliced off my thumbnail.

Believe me there isn't much fun in it, and the blood goes everywhere.

PIGGY BACKING.

You can also put a big shackle on the stock of your second anchor and slide it down the chain of the first one, until it lies on the bottom. Keep more or less the same tension on each chain. This is called piggy backing. When the boat tries to move astern, in a rising wind or choppy sea, and the weight comes onto the cable, it will dig the second anchor further in. The presence of the piggy backed anchor also ensures that the pull on the main anchor will be nearly horizontal, helping it dig in further rather than encouraging it to break out.

The motion of the boat will also be well damped. This is not so effective when the boat swings.

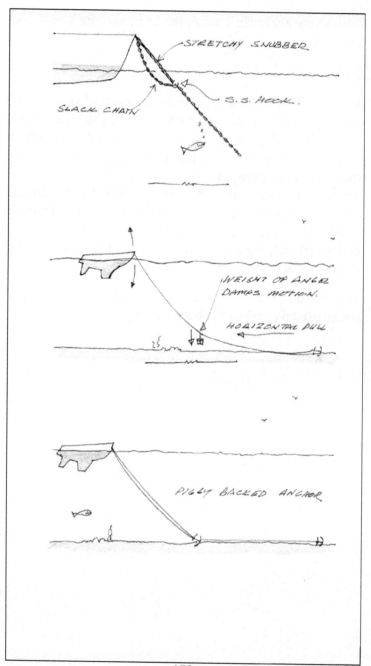

STRETCHY SNUBBER

SLACK CHAIN

S.S. HOOK.

WEIGHT OF ANGEL DAMPS MOTION.

HORIZONTAL PULL

PIGGY BACKED ANCHOR

BUOYING THE ANCHOR.

I never use an anchor buoy in a busy anchorage. It's something else you have to recover, and the chances are another boat coming in at night will run over it. In addition, it's very unlikely that the buoy will lie directly over your anchor at low water, so its value is, I believe, limited.

LETTING GO.

I am not going to try and tell you how to anchor. However, there are a few less obvious points to make which may help make your anchoring experience less stressful, both for you and for the other boats already there.

It's always interesting, and sometimes amusing, to watch another boat come into the anchorage, if you are sitting securely in your own spot. So, when you arrive as the newcomer, try and think ahead. This will avoid the need to go round and round the anchorage looking for a spot to settle and providing entertainment for the other yachts already there.

Go slowly. You are in the nautical equivalent of a car park. Avoid passing needlessly close to other boats, and when crossing, always pass round the stern and not close across the bows of boats already anchored. When you cross the bow of an anchored yacht you will be going slowly and more or less broadside on to the forces that are causing the other boat to lie the way she is, and the same forces will start to set you down onto her bow.

Remember once anchored you will wind up pointing in the same direction as the other boats that are already there, so take this into account.

If I am coming into an anchorage where there are likely to be coral heads, I usually go very slowly around the spot I hope to anchor in, to make sure my swinging circle is clear.

As a very general rule, I try and let the anchor go in line with, but off to one side of the stern of the boat I want to end up lying astern of. Unless you are stopped dead in calm water in which there is no current or tide it's worth remembering that you will probably be going astern when you let go, so the point at which you let the anchor go from the bow will not be the spot at which it lands on the sea bed. This is particularly significant in water greater than ten metres deep and when it is windy. In that situation I let about five metres of chain out, whilst still creeping ahead, then stop the boat and let the rest out once I can see she is going astern. That way I can then get the anchor on the bottom fast and drag out the chain, getting a near horizontal load on the anchor as soon as possible and encouraging it to dig in.

If there's enough room, I always put out chain equal to at least four times the depth of water I am anchoring in and often more. Unless you are in very shallow water indeed, three times the depth is not enough. There's no fun in waking in the middle of the night listening to the rising wind, feeling the motion of the boat and wishing you had more chain out. More chain at the start, less worry later.

Perhaps the most important rule is that you should always end up a safe distance from the other boats that are already there. There's no point in anchoring right on top of another boat, because all you will do is antagonise them and if you do start to drag you will have to move.

If you do end up close to another boat, it's courtesy to ask them if they are happy with you being there. If they are not, you must move. Similarly, if they let you see they are not happy without you asking, then don't argue. Give them a wave and move.

I sailed with one formidable South American lady who would simply stand at the bow of her boat and stare at the skipper of any boat she thought was getting too close. Words were seldom necessary.

On sand and rock, or coral or weed, it's always worth looking for a sandy patch on which to drop the anchor. After anchoring, if I am in clear and sufficiently shallow water, I like to get into the water with my fins and snorkel and check that the anchor is dug in, and not lying on its back. If it is, I swim down and turn it round the right way.

That done, I sit in the cockpit, open a beer and enjoy my surroundings.

HEAVING UP.

There two distinct phases to getting underway from an anchorage:

First of all heaving short, as it's called, when you wind in all the slack cable until the anchor is about to break out. Followed by a shorter second phase, during which you recover the remaining cable and the anchor. Until the anchor breaks out, you are anchored, but as soon as it's off the bottom you are underway, the boat is free of any restraint and circumstances can change rapidly.

Knowing the depth of water you are in, and the amount of chain you have out, it's a simple matter to know the point at which the anchor will break out. This is particularly important for a single-hander, because, unless it's glassy calm, as soon as the anchor comes free of the bottom the bow will try and blow down wind and you will need to take firm corrective action. When planning your departure, don't forget that the boat will come ahead as you start to heave in the chain, so the position at which she breaks out will be quite different to that at which you started heaving short.

If after heaving short you find yourself uncomfortably close to the stern of another boat, you might want to stop heaving in the chain, and go astern on the engine to drag the anchor out and to bring your boat back clear of the other one. Alternatively, the skipper of the other boat could give his boat a shear to one side, moving his stern away from its position above your anchor.

I usually go up to the bow and heave short using the forward footswitch. That way I can see exactly where the cable is leading. When I get to the point at which the anchor is still attached to the seabed, but only just, I go aft and complete the operation using the cockpit windlass control. That way I can immediately correct any tendency for the boat to fall off and go broadside to the wind. Unless it's very rough, you can safely motor slowly ahead with a bit of chain out if you really have to. It's better to risk putting a small mark on your bow than to wind up broadside across someone else's.

FOULED ANCHOR.

On occasion, you will heave short, then find that the anchor will not come free. This is more likely to happen in isolated anchorages than in those often used by cruising yachts. If you are anchored in some shallow spot with clear water, you will be able to see the problem, but under those circumstances you would have been able to see the bottom when you let the anchor go in the first place and probably wouldn't be in this mess now.

Usually you will not be able to see the anchor, so you will be working blind.

The usual reason that the anchor is fouled is that you have hooked into something on the bottom, such as an old mooring or some other piece of junk, or that the anchor has become jammed under a rock, or round a coral head. There are a few things you can try.

With an amount of chain out equal to just under twice the water depth, back off then motor ahead until the chain comes tight.

If that is no good:

Turn the boat through 180 degrees, and try and pull the anchor out in the opposite direction.

No luck? Keeping some weight on the chain, turn the boat in a slow circle around the anchor and try again. If that's no good, go back and do another circle in the opposite direction.

By this time you will probably notice other sailors watching smugly from their cockpits.

If you are hooked onto an old mooring or a piece of junk, it may be that there is sufficient power in your windlass to lift the anchor until it is either just below the surface, or better still on the surface. If you can achieve that, stop heaving, pass a line round the mooring wire or whatever it is you are attached to, then slack the anchor chain until the piece of line is taking the weight of the unwanted junk. Cut the line, stow the anchor and off you go.

If the windlass will lift the anchor and the obstruction off the bottom, but not raise it fully, it's worth pausing for ten

183

minutes or so. It may be that you are hooked into a piece of abandoned fishing gear or a mooring wire that has been sunk into the mud, and by pausing with the anchor chain tight, you give the gear, or the wire the chance to pull more of its length out of the mud and off the bottom, increasing the chances of being able to lift the anchor closer to the surface. The pause also gives the windlass a chance to cool down, decreasing the likelihood of burning out the motor. Not only that, if there is a sea causing the yacht to pitch, even a small amount, the natural buoyancy of the boat may help to pull the obstruction free.

It's always good to pause in mid problem, if you can. You aren't going anywhere in the short term anyway. If all else fails, put the anchor back on the bottom and look around for someone with scuba gear.

During my four year trip I hooked into quite a variety of odd things, including a waterlogged tree trunk, a few bits of rusty wire, an abandoned trawl board and a bundle of tangled steel rods of the kind used in the reinforcement of concrete. Thankfully, I always managed to get away.

CARING FOR THE CHAIN AND ANCHOR.

Anchor chain is usually mild steel which is galvanised. As a matter of course during its working life it is subject to much abuse, through contact with coral, rock, sand and stones, and through being stretched tight or stowed in a wet heap in a locker.

As a result, the galvanising will in time wear off and the portion of the chain which is most often in the water will show signs of rusting. The first forty metres or so closest to the anchor will get worn first. If you are anchoring a lot it is good practice to change the chain end for end after a couple of years so that the part which has spent nearly all its time in the locker and has had least use becomes the part in use, and the harder worked section is rested in the locker. I set off with a new anchor chain, and turned it end for end after three years. At the end of the trip the whole thing had had enough, and I replaced it.

Although there are some alloy anchors available, and some stainless, the majority are galvanised cast mild steel, like the chain. Anchors have a tough life. That is what they are designed for. I have never heard of an anchor wearing out, although I have seen one fail suddenly, when the shank fractured under load. That was due to a fault in the casting. A Bruce anchor has no moving parts, so there is nothing to fail, and really nothing to keep an eye on other than to look for signs of wear at the top eye, at the interface between the shank of the anchor and the shackle which attaches it to the chain.

At the end of my voyage the tips of the flukes on my anchor had rusted and I had the anchor re-galvanised.

It is worth using a stainless steel shackle to join the anchor to the chain, because it will always be easier to undo than a galvanised one. Don't forget to mouse the eye of the shackle pin with Monel wire so that it cannot turn. I never used a swivel, or any form of joining link. They are possible failure points.

There is a small eye on a Bruce, at the crown, and I keep a loop of line on it. That way I can reach down and grab the anchor with the boat hook if I want to lift it over the rail.

ANCHOR SIGNALS.

Many European countries insist on you showing an anchor ball during the day, and in some they will fine you if you don't. By day it's fairly obvious to other sailors whether a yacht is at anchor or moored to a buoy, because she will most likely have no sails up and will not be moving.

In any event, you should keep clear and avoid passing close ahead of her.

At night, it's a different matter and if you are coming into an anchorage from seaward, it can be very difficult to see anchored boats against a dark background, or their lights against a backdrop of shore lights. Always, always, show an anchor light at night, even if you are the only boat in the anchorage when the day ends. If you do not show a light and another boat runs into you, you do not have a leg to stand on, and it's likely that your insurer will lose no time in telling you so.

There is a fashion for some boats to hang a light over the cockpit, which is confusing. The anchor light should either be shown at the tip of the mast, which is not particularly effective, or forward of the mast a couple of metres off the deck, which is a much better indicator of the position of your bow, and being lower down is more easily seen from another boat under way.

Never, ever anchor in or right beside the fairway leading to a port, particularly a fishing port. Fishermen coming into port at night are trying to make a living and are invariably in a hurry. Often they will have deck lights on which reduce visibility. They have no interest in slowing down and trying to creep in avoiding anchored yachts, so stay well lit, and out of the way.

AND AT SEA...

I never leave the anchor on the bow during a sea passage, it is always brought aft, and stowed in the locker. There are two reasons for this. Firstly, you do not want any additional weight right at the bow during an open sea passage, because it will encourage pitching and will dampen the boat's ability to lift her bow to an oncoming sea.

Secondly, the anchor on a seven tonne yacht meeting an oncoming wave at six knots takes a big hit. No matter how well you lashed it in place before you left, it will start to move against it lashings. If the anchor starts to move, even a small amount, you must deal with the problem immediately. Going forward to re-lash it will be bad enough, but if it works free you could be in an even worse situation. You might be safer to bear away or run off before you go forward because if it is jumping about when you try to re-lash it, you will be putting your fingers in harm's way as you try to deal with it. It would probably be best to unshackle it and carry it down the deck, which is what you should have done before you left!

MOORING BUOYS.

You may, from time to time, want to make fast to a mooring buoy. It is quite unusual to come across a buoy with a pick up buoy attached to it. I carry a buoy lasso, which consists of a two metre length of 8mm chain with three metres of 12mm braid rope attached to each end. It makes life much easier for a single hander and you can easily make up your own lasso.

The weight of the chain makes it very easy to swing the loop over the buoy, and will draw the rope downwards on each side of it. Pull the rope tight and the chain will rise until it grips under the buoy, at which point you can make the rope tails fast on board. That will hold the boat securely and enable you to pass your slip line through the ring on top of the buoy at your leisure. Once you have done that, take the lasso off to avoid the chain damaging the buoy riser.

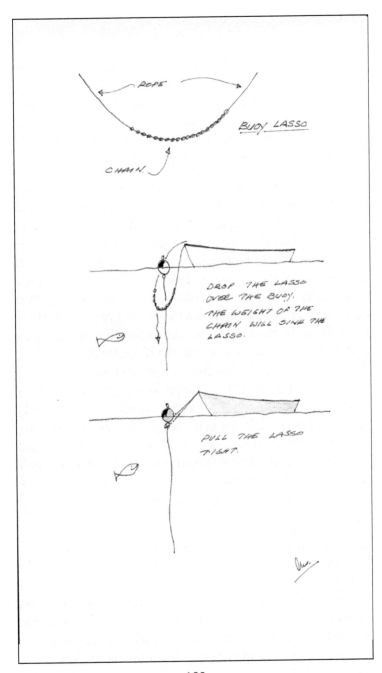

ROPE

BUOY LASSO

CHAIN.

DROP THE LASSO
OVER THE BUOY.
THE WEIGHT OF THE
CHAIN WILL SINK THE
LASSO.

PULL THE LASSO
TIGHT.

189

18. SAFETY EQUIPMENT.

A while ago I watched a sailing film shot in 1960, about one of the Clyde Cruising Club's iconic passage races. The skippers and crews wore jeans and sweaters, canvas sailing shoes and occasionally hats. The weather was moderate, no one wore a lifejacket and very few of the boats had lifelines. How times have changed!

When I got back home after my circumnavigation, I was struck by the number of training boats that were out and about. But even more surprising was the demeanour of the trainees on board. Even in fine weather, I would see them mustered on deck before dropping the mooring, looking like a squad of paratroopers about to be dropped into a war zone. Lifejackets, boots, oilskins, harnesses, hats, gloves and safety lines suggested that they were approaching their day sail on the basis that it was an expedition into a hostile and very dangerous environment. Of course the sea can be dangerous in certain conditions and having spent a large part of my life on it, I, as much as anyone, agree that it should be respected. But for goodness sake, there has to be some sort of middle ground. Let's teach people to enjoy the environment of sea, sky, wind and cloud within which they sail without starting from the premise that they should be frightened of it and that it is just waiting for the opportunity to cause them some horrible harm.

When I set off on what developed into my circumnavigation, I had just done the two-handed Round Britain and Ireland race and the boat was equipped to ISAF Category 1 so all the equipment I needed was on board, including a life raft, flares, Dan buoy, EPIRB and so on. In some ways this was a bit over the top for a single-handed cruise and I did occasionally wonder who was going to throw me the life ring if I fell over the side…

If you are setting off, you could spend thousands of pounds on safety equipment and end up with so much of it on board that its very presence poses a threat. I wouldn't put myself in the position of telling anyone whether they should carry a certain piece of equipment or not, it's entirely up to you.

For what it's worth, here is what I carried:

Four man life raft.

Flares

Grab bag, with extra flares, spare pair of specs, spare medication, portable GPS, extra water, etc.

EPIRB.

Personal Locator Beacon.

Lifebuoy and light.

Dan buoy light and flag.

Life-sling rescue system.

Two strobe lights.

Bolt cutters.

Throwing line.

Spare bungs.

Portable sail number.

Rescue knife.

Emergency torch.

Fire extinguishers.

Fire blanket.

KNIVES.

In an offshore race you are required to carry a rescue knife in a sheath, in the cockpit. You often see the sheath taped to something like the upright of the wheel support. That's all very well, but in an extreme situation it's liable to be rough, and the boat will be moving about a lot. The thought of someone drawing the knife from the sheath and then stumbling about the cockpit with it in their hand fills me with horror. If they slip they are liable to slash their hand badly or possibly injure someone else in the vicinity, adding to everyone's problems. I always had the sheathed knife within a holder of some sort. That way you can grab it and move to where it is needed, then take it out of its sheath. When I am cruising, I do not have a knife in the cockpit, but there is always one just inside the companionway along with a spike and a pair of pliers. If I need to go on deck in bad weather or at night, I never do so without a knife in my oilskin pocket.

LIFEJACKETS.

I do not wear a lifejacket as a matter of course when I am sailing. That is my choice, one I possibly make as a result of feeling completely at home on the water.

I do wear one if I am in a situation where it is best to clip on, because the jacket incorporates the harness to which I attach my strop.

I also wear one when I am in a situation where there is a heightened risk of falling overboard, such as when picking up a mooring single-handed, if it is choppy.

Modern lifejackets are so well designed that they are very easy to wear, even with a crotch strap attached.

SAFETY TRAINING.

There are a number of very good safety/survival courses available, and I think anyone setting off on a longish cruise would be well advised to attend one. An afternoon spent in full sailing gear in a swimming pool trying to get in and out of a life raft will teach you a lot.

CLOSING THOUGHTS.

On a well-run sensibly sailed boat, true emergencies are thankfully rare. As a cruise progresses and the months pass by, confidence builds, and inevitably the attention that is paid to safety issues tends to diminish as equipment lies unused and the pain of paying for it all becomes a distant memory. Before each ocean passage it is a good idea, even for a single-hander, to run through the inventory, do a mock raft deployment and get the flares out and re-read the operating instructions. You may be surprised by how much you have forgotten.

Safe sailing.

19. THINGS MECHANICAL.

The first boat I owned back in my early twenties had been built in 1902, and at some stage in her life she had been fitted with an auxiliary petrol engine, of a make now long defunct, and deservedly so. We tried everything in our power to get that thing to start, including pre–heating it with a blowlamp aimed directly into the carburettor and although it did burst into life on a couple of occasions it would never run for more than about half a minute. In those days it was common to sail on and off the mooring, or the anchor, and I soon got used to sailing in and out of harbours as well.

Times have changed and although there are cruising yachts which choose to rely solely on the wind in their sails to get around, they are few and far between. It may seem obvious to say that you need an engine, but it is only after many years of long distance voyaging that I have come to the firm conclusion that as well as being necessary, a reliable engine is the heart of any good cruising boat, particularly one that is sailed by just one, or possibly two people.

When I left Scotland, in 2010, Beyond still had her original engine By that time it was twenty years old and was starting to show signs of having had a difficult life. Although it never failed to start, there were problems with the alternator and the regulator circuits, and with the cooling system. By the time I had got down to the South coast of Portugal, I had already contributed generously to the financial well-being of several so called mechanical and electrical engineers, and I began to wonder if word of my charging problems was preceding me. By the time I arrived in the Caribbean the water pump had joined in the fun and was leaking on to the drive belt which in turn sprayed the water on to the alternator. I rigged an empty soup can under the pump to catch the drips before they landed on the belt, but this only allowed me to run for about seven minutes before the can had to be emptied.

In Saint Lucia, when I tried to get a replacement pump the dealer pointed out several other potential age-related failures, and persuaded me that to expect to transit the Canal and sail across the Pacific without major mechanical problems would be expecting a miracle. I dug deep into my little pot of savings and replaced the engine. I have never regretted it. I also upgraded the folding prop from two to three blades, which gave me more speed for the same revolutions and much more thrust when manoeuvring. I loved my new engine and treated it like royalty.

PROPULSION AND POWER.

We all know that on a cruising yacht the engine provides propulsion via the propeller and electrical power from its alternator. Some cruising yachts have a stand-alone generator, with which they can charge their batteries and provide power to other electrical equipment such as the windlass, but many do not. Without wanting to state the obvious, it's worth remembering that the requirements of propulsion and the provision of electrical power are separate but linked.

PROPULSION.

Perhaps the most obvious function of the engine is that it will keep you moving when there is no wind, and will get you in and out of port when it is too awkward to sail.

At some time or another you will inevitably hit a calm patch, which, on the open ocean, could last for days or weeks. Without an engine you have no choice other than to drift. But it won't be a calm and peaceful experience, because there is always a swell, which will keep you rolling about and will in time become intolerable. You will have to wait for the wind to come to you, and it could be a long time coming, because on the ocean most areas of persistent calm are seasonal. How long have you got?

With an engine you can idle along at low revolutions, making slow but steady progress towards your destination and out of the calm area. I usually let the engine run at about 1700 RPM, which gets me just over a hundred miles a day in flat water and burns less than two litres of fuel an hour.

In the tropics, particularly around reefs and islands, the wind often falls very light in the evening and may not start to blow again until a few hours after dawn, so if you find yourself arriving somewhere in the evening without an engine, you could well be in a fix. Very often there are strong currents running in these areas and not only would you be unable to make sufficient progress to get in, it could be that the current will be setting you on to the reef and it's likely that you will be unable to anchor because the sea bed rises almost vertically at the drop off outside the reef. At best you may find yourself being carried away from your destination by the current. That would be a little discouraging if you had just spent weeks getting there. Not only that, you would have to beat back up to the island next day before you could try and sail in through the boat pass again. The passes into many lagoons are tricky enough under power, and would be very difficult under sail, so the lack of an engine could render a few of the islands inaccessible, and the less accessible islands often make the best destinations.

At the other end of the scale, in some areas, particularly those close to developed ports, you may not be allowed to sail at all. This is certainly the case at the Panama Canal. I arrived there from Curacao with a fishing net round the prop, which rendered my shiny new engine useless and meant that I had to sail in through the breakwater in amongst all the shipping entering and leaving. A difficult situation made worse by having to listen to the wrath of the Port Control station, which came over the radio telling me that I must stop sailing immediately and use my engine.

Having got through that little difficulty and into a quieter area, I then had to sail into a strange marina, and get the boat alongside unaided. My safe arrival beer changed its status from being a pleasure to being a medical necessity.

There is another very strong safety argument for having a reliable engine, particularly if you are single-handed. If you are in an anchorage and it comes on to blow and you start to drag, are you really going to be able to get sail on and beat out into open water, while getting the anchor up and stowed? You would need a lot of luck.

No matter how good a sailor you are, if things start to get difficult, swallow your pride and press the button.

POWER.

You can have a wind generator and an array of solar panels to provide a slow charge to your batteries, but the sun does not always shine and the wind does not always blow. Even when operating well, these will only provide a few amps. Probably sufficient to keep your batteries up and run lights and a fridge, but certainly not enough to allow you to run anything with a heavy current load like a windlass. So the engine and its alternator become an essential team, both to provide low amp battery top up, via the regulator, and a constant charge able to meet the high amp demands of something like a windlass, which when heaving up the anchor can draw as much as 60 amps. Try that, without your engine providing constant high amp charge, and you will probably wreck your batteries. Then what? Modern engines do not have starting handles.

TAKE CARE OF IT.

Unlike my old, rusty, horizontally opposed piece of scrap, modern marine diesels, if looked after, are very reliable indeed. There are plenty of books on the subject, but the kind of routine maintenance you can do yourself revolves around cleanliness of the fuel, keeping the coolant levels up, changing the oil, fuel and water filters and the oil at regular intervals, and routinely checking belt tension and so on. Cleanliness, as they say, is next to Godliness. It's easy to do but very important. Always carry spare fuel and oil filters, spare belts, and at least sufficient lubricating oil to make one complete oil change, with a bit to spare. Level and tension checks became part of the Saturday routine, and I always found it to be a real pleasure. It was a piece of preventative maintenance, which once done, was likely to have a very positive effect. The original arrangement for the engine had a water trap and pre-filter between the tank and the engine. It was the type with a glass bowl under the filter. It was almost inaccessible and changing the filter was a real pain in the butt. In South Africa I replaced it with a Racor type trap and filter, which I fitted above and just behind the engine, with a shut off valve on each side of it. Changing filters became a pleasure. In four years of voyaging I never once had problems with dirty fuel or fuel

198

that contained water. It may just have been luck, but I doubt it.

TRANSFERRING FUEL.

Unless you have big tanks, you will probably carry some spare diesel in jerry cans. Transferring the contents of the cans into the tank can be a problem, because on many boats the filler is out on the side deck and you will almost certainly be doing the transfer at sea, when there will be some motion. I used a 'jiggle syphon'. They are not expensive and make the job very easy. Another tip, don't empty the can completely, unless you are really desperate. If you do, you risk transferring any sludge or dirt that has settled in the bottom of the can.

If you do run out of fuel and the engine stops, always change the fuel filter at the first available opportunity afterwards.

COOLING WATER.

No matter how good your engine is, you cannot run it without cooling water.

You cannot pump cooling water without a working impeller in your pump. If your pump is belt driven, you need a belt as well. So, no belt or no impeller, no engine. Carry spares. The fresh water cooling side of my engine gave no problems, and I rarely if ever had to top up the coolant but I suffered some difficulties on the salt water side due to the sea water intake holes in the sail drive housing becoming clogged. I got round this by installing a traditional salt water intake in the hull and drawing water through this. I also replaced the rubber hose between the pump and the tube stack with one made of clear material. That way you can see if there are any bubbles. If there are, you are drawing air somewhere and probably not delivering enough water to the tube stack.

When you change the impeller, or open the pump to check it, take a look at the back of the face plate. It may be worn. A temporary solution is to turn it round and re-fasten it with the inner face outwards. I always changed the gasket when I removed the face plate.

One last thing about impellers. You will be able to buy cheap impellers, badged as being suitable for x,y, or z-type engines. In my experience it's not worth it. By the time you discover that they don't fit properly it will be too late. I buy genuine spares, two at a time, so that I always have a spare.

If you have a good impeller, pump and belt and you are still suffering from lack of cooling water, check the water filter. If the filter is clear, you possibly have drawn something over, or partially into, the water intake on the hull. When the engine is running, the suction provided by the pump will help hold the obstruction in place, particularly if it's a bit of plastic bag. Stopping the engine will stop the suction and your problem may just float away. If not, you can disconnect the pipe at the intake filter and blow down it, either by mouth, or with the dinghy pump. If all else fails close the seacock and try and rig up a separate source of cooling water. If you have enough hose, you could take a line from the galley saltwater pump inlet or the toilet inlet. It might not provide enough volume for full speed operation but it could be sufficient to let you run at slow speed, which is better than nothing.

Always make sure the shut-offs on skin fittings are free to operate, that the jubilee clips on the hoses are in good condition and that you have spare hose and spare clips. I used to operate all the seacocks as part of my weekly checks.

One final thing on the subject of cooling. Try and let the engine warm up for a few minutes before you ask it to do any work and let it run at tick over for a few minutes after you have finished with it so that its internal parts cool down gradually. If the engine has been working hard, the block and water jacket will be at high working temperature. If you suddenly stop the flow of cooling water the internal temperature of the engine will immediately rise with possible boiling off of the residual cooling water, known as after boiling.

If the high temperature alarm on your engine goes off, you are on the threshold of doing some damage if you don't shut the engine down, or at least slow to a tick over. I installed a temperature sensor probe into the rubber exhaust just behind the exhaust elbow, with a temperature gauge and alarm at the chart table. I soon got to know that the reading would be about 34 degrees, and set the alarm threshold just a couple of degrees above that. I glance at it occasionally when the engine is running, but I know that my additional alarm will give very early warning of any problems, before the engine's own alarm sounds.

A good rough indicator of engine cooling efficiency is to lower a bucket over the side and collect a little water from the exhaust outlet. You should be able to comfortably put your hand in it.

I also know that at normal revs I can comfortably put my hand on top of the engine. Not very scientific, but that's the way they used to do it before gauges became the norm.

BILGE PUMPS.

The bigger manual bilge pumps are very efficient, but their operation depends on manpower. If you are single-handed and you have water coming in, you cannot be pumping the water out and locating, then solving, the problem at the same time.

I installed a high capacity electrical pump capable of shifting thirty litres per minute out of the bilge. It has its own dedicated discharge and a power supply that can be controlled either automatically via a float switch, or manually. The pump is located outside the bilge and just level with the waterline.

My thinking was that if I got into trouble with water coming in, I could start the engine and the pump and just let it get on with pumping while I got on with solving the problem. The pump would take care of the water level and the engine would keep feeding the batteries to keep pace with the current draw that the pump was creating. The heart of the boat, right enough.

The bilges on Beyond remained dry and thankfully I never had to use the pump in anger, but I used to run it once a week. I would pour a couple of buckets of sea water into the bilge, add some washing up liquid and run the pump. That way the bilge gets freshened up, and the soapy solution helps lubricate the impeller in the pump. Another satisfying Saturday job.

20. THE DREADED AMP.

SIMPLICITY.

I don't know much about electricity. Over the years I have tried to read several learned books on the subject of electricity on board, some of them very well-known indeed. With the exception of one, I have found them all to be over complicated. I have come to the conclusion that you can get by as long as you keep it simple and have a basic knowledge of how a 12 V DC circuit works. Even I can handle that.

When I bought Beyond, much of her wiring was shambolic. Bits had been added in and others changed around over the years and although most of it worked, it was very hard to follow the system. There was one clue, however. Where the cables left the heel of the mast and entered the junction box someone had pencilled a note which read "the old red is now the brown". Very helpful.

BACK TO BASICS.

During those early months I paid a boat electrician to start at the batteries and renew everything, running a high amp positive and negative cable to separate negative and positive bus bars behind the switchboard. He also put in a shunt, (don't ask) and replaced the wiring to the engine starter motor and the alternator.

On this solid foundation, I then built a complete new panel, with a very up market relay board, and connected that to a new connecting bar. It was easy work requiring very little real technical knowledge, just the ability to cut wire and attach crimped terminals, something I enjoyed doing. I knew then that everything as far as that bar was brand new and okay. After a fair bit of detective work and trial and error I was able to connect up all the existing wiring from the lights, etc, to the connector bar. To my great satisfaction it all worked. New instruments and some new equipment have followed over the years, but knowing everything on the supply side was 100 % has made their installation easy.

A lot of boats are fitted with just a small analogue voltmeter to indicate the state of the batteries. These small meters are hard to read and provide very little information. That was all I had to start with. I replaced it with a digital battery monitor with a big read out, which gives me an immediate and accurate measurement of the state of charge of the batteries, the current consumption when under load and the amount of charge they are taking when the engine is running. I have come to know what loads to expect under normal operating conditions and can tell at a glance if there is something amiss.

The only test equipment I carried was a simple analogue multi-meter and a test bulb with about a metre of twin-core cable attached, with crocodile clips at the end. I also had a crimping tool, cable snips, pliers and a gas powered soldering iron, plus lots of connectors, insulating tape and spare cable, etc.

On Beyond, I had two 120 amp hour sealed batteries for the domestic circuits, and one 70 amp hour wet cranking battery for the engine. I had to replace the engine battery after a year, because I allowed it to run dry. The main batteries lasted three years and were still fairly good, according to the tester in South Africa, but I replaced them anyway before going round the Cape and heading up to Brazil, because they were available and cheap. Sealed batteries are the answer. I soon learned to keep the terminals and posts clean, that even a tightly fastened terminal can work loose and that it only takes the slightest degree of looseness to create a complete failure of the supply. If I ever have a problem with something drawing high amps, such as the engine failing to turn over when the starter is pressed, I go straight to the battery and check the tightness of the terminals. Stick to the basics and check them first.

LIGHTENING THE LOAD.

I replaced the bulbs on all the internal lights, and in the masthead tricolour light with LED bulbs. These days the only lights with the old fashioned squirrel cage type of bulbs are the steaming lights, and although they draw a relatively high amount of current they are only ever on when the engine is running, so they are not a problem.

I had one LED strip light located over the chart table which was wired directly to the batteries by-passing the main switch panel. The idea being that if there was a problem with the panel during the night hours I could use the directly wired light to help me see what I was doing. This light drew so little power that it could be left on all night, providing a helpful source of light on the not infrequent occasions at sea, or at anchor, when I need to get up in a hurry.

CHARGING.

When I set off I was completely reliant on the engine to charge the batteries. I do not like wind generators, they are noisy and pretty inefficient when you are sailing downwind anyway. The wind-vane was steering the boat and I didn't use lights much at night, other than the navigation lights, so all was well. That was until I got into the tropics and the fridge started to run for prolonged periods to cope with the high ambient temperature, forcing me to run the engine in the evening and again first thing in the morning. In the Caribbean I replaced the cable between the batteries and the fridge with a brand new high quality tinned twin cable which could probably have carried enough current to light most of the bars in Grenada. That really helped. I also installed a 60 Watt solar panel and that made a great difference too. I loved my panel, no moving parts, maintenance free, and requiring only sunlight to produce electricity.

I arranged things so that the panel could be tilted to maximise the available sunlight and it worked well until I got to Darwin. There, the diodes in the small plastic box behind the panel quit, because of corrosion, and the panel started to empty the batteries instead of charging them. These diode boxes at the back of panels are a source of weakness, and you need to smear all the edges with silicone to keep the damp out. I bought a new panel when mine quit and then a friend from another boat showed me how to mend the first one with a couple of diodes bought from a radio shop. A few minutes with the soldering iron and I wound up with two working panels. My charging capacity had doubled and for the next couple of years I rolled along happily without ever worrying about lack of power.

IN PORT.

For the odd occasion when I was alongside I had a small charger wired into the shore power system which cut in automatically when something like the fridge started up at night and put a load on the batteries. It ran almost silently, and I derived a certain pleasure from the knowledge that I would waken with the batteries as well charged as they had been when the previous day's setting sun had stopped charging them.

INVERTER.

I also had an inverter, wired directly to the batteries, which provided me with a 220 V supply allowing me to charge the laptop and other low amperage items. It became poorly on one occasion when a lady guest plugged in a hair dryer, but thankfully it recovered.

DON'T WORRY, BE HAPPY.

One thing I have learned about electricity, is that when you only have a small amount of knowledge there is a tendency to worry too much, particularly when you are tired, creating, in your mind, a problem that does not actually exist.

In my limited experience, in about 90 percent of cases, with a basic 12 V system, faults can be traced to a poor connection somewhere in the circuit. Possibly as simple as a slightly loose terminal at the battery, which is a good place to start checking.

On one solo Atlantic crossing, I became suspicious that my batteries were not charging properly. I only had an analogue voltmeter with a very small dial in the system, and in fact it was hard to tell what was really going on, but I 'traced' the problem to the chart table light, which I wrongly blamed for draining the current. It was the middle of the night, but I decided to take immediate action, opened up the switch panel, and with a pair of pliers cut through the twin cable leading to the light. Bang! There was a blue flash, and a puff of smoke as the pliers shorted the positive and negative sides of the wire and set the insulation on fire. The batteries must have been okay after all.

THE LITMUS TEST...

Do the lights go on? Yes. Does the battery turn the engine over? Yes.

Stop worrying.

21. IT'S A GAS.

On one of my previous boats I had a spirit stove, which I enjoyed using, because of its cleanliness. When I was making my way around the world I met up with a couple of boats who were using spirit stoves, but the majority of ocean cruising boats that I met with, used bottled gas, as I did. Before I left, I was given all sorts of dire warnings about the dangers of using the wrong type of gas, I was told that either the water wouldn't boil because there wouldn't be enough heat, or the boat would blow up, or possibly both. The fact is, that when you are on the other side of the world, where some countries use butane and some use propane, you make do with whatever you can get your bottles filled up with. In fact, it turned out that it was the bottles and the regulators that were the problem, not the gas. I set off with the usual 3.5kg Camping Gaz blue bottles which are in common use in Europe, and I was able to swop or get them filled everywhere I went, until I got to New Zealand.

In the Caribbean there is a strong American influence and all the chandlers sell American style bottles. Some of these are now made transparent, so that you can see exactly how much gas you have left. It was noticeable that nearly all the American boats carried their bottles out on deck, or secured to the push pit rail, rather than in a locker. I liked the idea of these, but they wouldn't fit my locker, and I don't like carrying stuff on deck so I carried on with my own outfit of blue Gaz bottles.

I had no problems topping up in the canal zone, and set off across the Pacific with all my bottles full. Generally, when

I am on my own, I get between ten and twelve days out of one bottle depending on how much I use the oven. I tend to drink a lot of tea and coffee, and in the tropics, when I have only one cooked meal a day, it's the kettle that uses most of the gas. Much of the Pacific is heavily influenced by France, and so there was no problem getting my blue bottles filled in Polynesia.

In Tonga, the availability of gas depended on the arrival of the store ship, which carried a large tank on board and pumped its contents ashore into the local tank farm. This happened once every ten days or so, and the event triggered an immediate gathering of cruisers with empty bottles eager to get them filled before stocks ran out again. I joined the throng one day and turned up with my blue bottles, but the guy at the filling point didn't have an adaptor that would fit them. With typical Tongan inventiveness and goodwill he punctured a hole in a piece of cardboard and put that between his adaptor and the bottle to form a rough seal. He then held the adaptor down and added more weight by sitting on it, before opening the valve, at which point a cloud of gas shot up the leg of his shorts. But he just laughed and kept at it until the gauge told him the bottle was full and then gave it back to me. I am not sure what his wife would have had to say about it when he got home.

That got me as far as New Zealand, where the whole situation changed. When I took my, by now well-travelled and slightly rusted, blue bottles into the depot, and laid them on the counter, the man in charge almost called the bomb squad. Not only did he refuse to fill them he wanted to take them out of circulation, on the grounds that they were a hazard to public safety. In the end I was allowed to take them away, but the only way I could carry on cooking was to buy two new, tested, certified and stamped New Zealand bottles and a regulator to match. New Zealand is a very heavily regulated country and the man who fills your bottle handles the task as if he was dealing with nuclear waste. On go the gauntlets, goggles and safety hat, and that's just to check the date and test stamp on the base. If you get past that stage, you get the gas, but they do everything but sound a siren and clear the area before they even approach the valve. I wondered what they would think of Tongan safety procedures?

The New Zealand bottles got me up to New Caledonia, where, being a part of France, blue bottles were again in vogue. So, when I got there, I put my remaining full New Zealand bottles into deep reserve, and brought out the blues.

That got me as far as Australia. But once I got there, more problems arose. They certainly didn't like the blue bottles, but they didn't accept the New Zealand ones either. One of my New Zealand bottles was empty, and I needed them both for the Indian Ocean crossing. By good fortune I was lucky enough to find someone who would fill it, as long as I didn't tell anyone. He clearly didn't want to be raided by the gas police.

Onwards to Mauritius with my now growing international collection of bottles; only to find that in Mauritius, despite the French influence, they wouldn't touch the blue bottles, or the New Zealand ones. I was now running on empty, so back to the nearest hardware store where I bought two of the biggest Mauritian bottles that would fit into my locker, plus of course, a new regulator to fit them, and a new spanner to fit the regulator. Every time I changed regulators I took care of the connection between the regulator and my system by the simple expedient of unscrewing the clips on the rubber tube and re-attaching it to the new regulator. Not being a certificated gas fitter, with proof-tested clips, a printed method statement, a risk assessment and of course an 'internationally approved' screwdriver, it was a wonder I didn't blow myself up and the nearby boats with me. But I guess I was just lucky. A couple of months later I arrived in South Africa, which as you won't be surprised to hear, didn't accept Mauritian bottles, or New Zealand ones, nor of course the good old blue ones, which, by now, had assumed international pariah status.

So, off to gas land again for a couple of South African bottles, another spanner and a new regulator. By now the rubber hose was coming off and on with the ease of an old hat, and I soon had the whole thing connected up and the kettle whistling happily once again. But a problem was looming. I had no room for all the now useless bottles!
How do you get rid of empty gas bottles? You can't throw them over the side, and you can hardly chuck them in a skip in case they wind up in an incinerator and explode. So I took to leaving them lying around, in the hope that some passer-by might take them away, and my progress round the various ports on the South African coast was marked by a trail of discarded cylinders. Once I was back in the Atlantic, "les bleus" came back into fashion, but it was in the Caribbean, back where it had all started, that I suffered the unkindest cut of all, because I found a place that would have filled my big, brand new, red Mauritian bottles, now sadly abandoned somewhere in South Africa.

Perhaps I should have stuck to alcohol after all. I will know better next time.

22. STAYING SAFE.

Reading some cruising books could give you the impression that you will be living in a state of constant fear, and that you should barricade yourself down below every night when anchored or alongside in a marina. There are certain parts of the world where cruising boats are at greater risk than others, but word soon gets round, incidents are widely reported on the radio net and these areas can be avoided. But accounts vary. I was told by locals to stay well away from the bays at the North end of the island of St Vincent, in the Caribbean, yet I met a number of boats who stopped there and had no problems at all. In some areas of the Caribbean, such as St Lucia, Grenada and Martinique, where cruising boats provide a huge income for local businesses, it was said that the locals themselves try and keep things under control, fearing that the boats will stop coming. The best approach is simply to exercise common sense. Anyone who walks around alone after dark in Panama or in the South African ports, or on some of the Caribbean Islands only has themselves to blame if things go wrong. If the local advice is to stay inside the marina at night, or not to go ashore from the anchorage after dark then you should follow it. I always did.

In four years of voyaging, I had two items stolen from the boat. In New Zealand I carelessly left a pair of binoculars in the cockpit when I went ashore, and they were taken, and in French Polynesia I lost a pair of flip flops which I left in the dinghy.

I had my credit card stolen in South Africa, whilst in the lobby of the bank, and that was my own fault because I ignored the advice we had been given about how to stay safe when using an ATM.

That was it. No one boarded the boat without permission, no one attacked me, and nothing was ever vandalised. I did hear of a number of incidents involving other boats, including two fatalities, so perhaps I was just lucky.

In Fiji, I bought an ironwood axe handle, which I kept down below. It was heavy but it was nicely balanced, and I still have it. Whether or not I would have had the time, or space to wield it to any real effect is open to question! I also kept an empty washing up liquid bottle filled with diesel oil. If you squirt that in someone's eyes, it completely disables them because their eyes immediately close up. Quite what you do next, would, I suppose, depend on the circumstances. I had a standard latch on my hatch-boards and locked the coach-roof hatches from below. There were no metal grids, screeching alarm systems, or recordings of growling dogs. But perhaps as a rather shabbily dressed old Scot I was a less than tempting target.

HIDE AND SEEK.

I carried about eighty books on Beyond and I cut a square recess in the pages of one so that I could put valuables inside the book, then place it in amongst all the others. I kept my passport, my Rolex, my credit cards and about two hundred US dollars there when I was in port. I also had three or four old and useless credit cards which I kept in the top drawer under the chart table along with some local currency. Most water thieves will go straight for the top drawer, because that is where most people put their stuff when they empty their pockets, and I hoped that if anyone did get down below they might just grab what was there and go.

CASUAL CREW.

In many places where cruising boats gather there will be young people looking for crewing jobs. In the Atlantic area many are trying to hitch a ride over to the Caribbean. The gates to some of the harbours in the Canaries are festooned with handwritten advertisements and whilst the people who have written them all say they can cook and will work hard, it is pretty clear that most of them have no idea of what is involved in crewing and living on a small sailing boat. Some are known to have arrived alongside with a large back pack, a surfboard and a guitar. Collapsible bicycles are not unknown. In the Caribbean there are more eager sailors, but at least they will already have made it that far, and will presumably have a reasonable idea of how to get along and make a useful contribution to life on board. In the Pacific Islands there were fewer 'floating' crew folk, and those that were there had already come a great distance and tended to be better organised with cards, contact details, and the offer to provide references.

Whilst I was in Fiji I took on one such person, because I was on my own and it was too dangerous to try and get in and out of some of the anchorages I wanted to visit without someone on the bow watching for coral heads. I had already come across her in a previous port and she was a fairly well known member of the cruising community. We agreed on the ground rules right at the start, and spent a few days in the harbour at Vuda Point before setting off. We visited the Immigration office, signed her on to my manifest, and I took control of her passport. Over the couple of weeks during which we cruised we were never more than a day sail from the next island and if things had started to go wrong it would have been easy to end the arrangement. In fact it worked out very well.

If you do think about taking someone on to voyage to a different country, you need to consider what will happen when you arrive there and they will have to clear Immigration. If the authorities at your destination won't accept your shipmate, you could be in a mess, particularly if you want to get them off the boat. In any event, you will be responsible for them whilst they are there, and you need to keep a hold of their passport, so that if they do go adrift, as does happen, you can then hand their ID over to the authorities. If they simply jump ship, taking their passport with them, you will be considered to have aided their illegal entry to the country. In some areas of the Pacific, such as the French administered islands, Fiji, Tonga and so on, the authorities have become fed up with dealing with those who outstay their welcome. The days of the starry-eyed dreamers who dropped in, dropped out and lived on the beach are long gone.

But it is not all one sided. On a few occasions I came across crew who had become completely disillusioned with their skippers.

Amongst our little itinerant sailing community was a boat which seemed to be experiencing more than its fair share of difficulties. Her skipper, a retired gentleman from Scandinavia, had done a course which, I believe, allowed him to sail off and take paying crew with him, on the basis that they could do the trip and learn how to sail. Arriving in Cocos, he eventually, after some difficulty managed to sail into the lagoon. His lady crew, who was also Scandinavian, headed straight for another boat, explaining, "I have been on that boat for a month. I may not know much about sailing, but I know enough to know that that useless b.....d knows f.... all!"

THE THREAT OF PIRACY.

Acts of piracy against yachts certainly do occur. Despite the fact that the areas of the world where they are a real problem are well documented, and that it is perfectly possible to make a circumnavigation without entering them, yachts still go there. It's a mystery to me.

When on passage, my anti-piracy strategy was firstly to avoid the high risk areas altogether and secondly, I planned to offer no resistance whatsoever if I was boarded. I kept a small hand held GPS hidden away and the idea was just to let the boarders take whatever they wanted in the hope that they would leave me alive and able to make my way to land somewhere. Thankfully the plan was never put to the test.

FIREARMS.

I know of quite a few boats, mostly from the USA, who carried firearms on board, I never did. Those who were armed made strong arguments in favour of their approach, one being that they always kept a gun in their house, or car, when at home. Those who did not carry arms could put the opposite case just as convincingly but it was not something that cruisers spent much time talking about.

Apart from the fact that you must declare any weapon, including a spear gun, when you arrive, you have to land the items ashore into custody and you are only allowed to retrieve them just before departure. So the sense of protection that their firearms provided was only available to the boats that carried them when they were at sea. One assumes that there isn't very much to shoot at on the open ocean, and the tragic incident which led to the death of Sir Peter Blake suggests that the chances of coming through any piracy incident in one piece are greatly reduced if you offer armed resistance.

23. STAYING WELL.

Ocean voyaging on a sailing boat is a very healthy way of life. I set off on my voyage after two years of desk bound work running a fairly stressful project. I came back four years later, feeling much fitter and looking much better than I had when I left. I had developed a lot of upper body strength through hoisting and trimming sails, rowing the dinghy and lugging jerry cans of fuel and water around. Also my leg muscles had become much stronger as a result of the continual tensing and relaxing they had been doing to compensate for the motion of the boat at sea, and the work they had been doing in climbing up and down into the cockpit many times each day and walking everywhere when I was ashore.

Additionally, I had been living largely outdoors in sunny climates, not drinking much alcohol and eating a very healthy, low fat, diet. All these factors combined with sunshine and the very low levels of day to day stress worked together to keep me feeling well.

In my book, 'The Long Way Home', there is a photograph of myself and four of my ocean sailing friends, taken at the Simonstown Yacht Club in Natal. At the time of the photo four of us were solo sailors on circumnavigations and four of us were within a year of our seventieth birthdays. We look well and we look happy. Ocean sailing is certainly good for you.

SOME ROUTINES.

There are a few routine precautions that you should take. You must drink enough water each day to avoid de-hydration and to keep your internal plumbing flushed through. I worked on two litres a day, plus whatever I took in the form of tea and coffee. Water on its own is a bit dull, so I used to make up a litre bottle of water with lime juice in it and keep it in the fridge. You will be able to tell from the colour of your urine whether you are drinking enough water. Clear is good, yellow is not.

You must do what you can to protect your skin from the sun. At the start of a voyage you need to build up a tan slowly, and that in itself will help protect you. In day to day sailing, your face, neck, shoulders and arms are vulnerable. You need a hat with a big brim, a bandana for your neck and a pair of board shorts with legs that come down below the knee, to protect your thighs when you are sitting down.

I was in the habit of sailing in bare feet, so my feet got very brown and the soles became very tough.

Ashore, I always wore deck shoes or flip flops.

I did not wear sailing gloves, instead allowing my hands to gradually harden up to the extent that I didn't need gloves anyway.

You will need plenty of sunscreen.

I have seen many cruising boats with very complicated and extensive biminis and cockpit awnings or framed canopies to keep out the sun, and I know of a few, on board which the protective canopies were so extensive, that their crews could not see the mainsail from the cockpit. I often thought that if they had such a horror of the sun they might have been better staying at home. I could not rig a bimini on Beyond when I was sailing, because of the location of the mainsheet; but I did have a big hat.

In port, I rigged an awning over the boom which created a large area of shade in the cockpit.

I developed a growth on the back of my right hand as a result of exposure to the sun. I had it surgically removed and the biopsy showed it to be harmless. The worst bit of the whole thing was getting the stitches out.

It is in the nature of your daily life on board that you will spend a lot of time gazing at the horizon. There is a continual glare from the sea and you must wear eye protection, something I did not do enough. Cheap sunglasses are a trap, because the coating on the lenses can become cracked or fail over a very small area, which has the effect of concentrating the light at one spot on your eye. You need good sunglasses and you need to look after them.

INSECTS.

In port whether alongside or at anchor, you will receive visits from a variety of flying insects, particularly in the evening, when they will be attracted to the lights on board.

I found, in general, that the larger the insect was, the easier it was to deal with and although they do not make ideal companions most are harmless. Some of the smaller ones can be very hard to see and often your only warning that there is a mosquito down below will be when you hear the characteristic high pitched whine it makes in flight. However, as long as it's whining, it's flying. Your problems start when the whining stops, because it has landed, probably on you. You do not feel a mosquito bite you, often the first sign that it has done so is when you waken in the morning with a few itchy lumps on your wrists or ankles, or whatever other part of you that has been left exposed outside whatever it is you have been sleeping under. Mosquitos seem to prefer the thinner skin around wrists and ankles, it is unusual to be bitten elsewhere.

Whatever you do, do not scratch a mosquito bite, it will almost certainly turn septic. This happened to me in the Caribbean and I had to get help from a doctor ashore.

If you do get an infected bite, pour some hydrogen peroxide on it. It fizzes and stings a bit, but it's very effective in neutralizing poisons.

Sleeping under a mosquito net may have a certain romantic feel to it, but it is far from convenient. The best way to prevent problems is to have screens over the hatches. I made some and they worked very well, keeping the bugs out whilst allowing me to leave the hatches open and still let the air in.

You will need plenty of insect spray, both for flying insects, which is a fine spray, and for crawlers, which is usually thicker. Keep them in a handy spot. It is easy to grab the wrong aerosol in the dark. I did on one occasion and found myself trying to shoot down a mosquito with a can of WD 40. I would have been better throwing the can at it.

There was quite a bit of discussion amongst we sailors about the wisdom of taking anti-malarial drugs. I never did, although I was never in a high risk area.

Finally, if you are anchored and you see a rain squall approaching from the land, prepare for an invasion. Very often the wind that precedes such a squall will blow dozens of insects ahead of it.

GALLEY AND FOOD ROUTINES.

In the tropics, you must keep the galley area spotless, especially if you are preparing meat or fish, both of which will attract bluebottles. In the Polynesian islands, there is a particularly unpleasant and persistent shiny blue fly, which can smell fish a mile off. It wasn't unusual to have to put in all the hatch boards if I was cutting up fish.

Similarly, don't leave fish scraps in your bin. If you can, empty the garbage at the end of every day and pour a little bleach down the sink drain, followed by a kettle full of boiling water.

If you buy vegetables from a market or roadside stall ashore, wash them thoroughly in a bucket of fresh water with a spoonful of bleach in it, preferably before they come aboard and certainly before they go down below. Some time, just for interest buy a bunch of bananas from a stall ashore and dangle them over the side. You will be surprised to see what swims out.

If you are buying provisions from a store, remove any cardboard wrapping, particularly if it is corrugated, before you stow the items that have been wrapped in it. Corrugated cardboard is a favourite lurking place for insect eggs, and you could be welcoming a complete generation of cockroaches on board.

I carried some water purification tablets, but I did not ever have a problem with the fresh water I got from ashore, even in remote areas, although I would always flush the tanks through when I got back to civilisation. In countries where it was available I bought bottled water for drinking with the lime juice, but I never relied on it exclusively.

223

Most boats carry their own fresh water hose with a selection of end fittings. If you are shipping water through a marina or dockside hose, always run the water for a few minutes to flush the hose through, before you put it in the tank.

BASIC FIRST AID.

I carried three first aid kits. A very expensive sealed kit, approved for use on charter vessels, a less exotic kit 'offshore' approved, and a Tupperware food storage box packed with Elastoplast, disinfectant, antiseptic cream, zinc oxide tape, Steri-Strip plastic stitches, and so on.

The sealed kit remained sealed and was thrown out after four years because it was out of date, the 'Offshore' kit was opened once, so that I could use the tweezers to help mend a small electrical unit, and the Tupperware box saw plenty of use.

The most important thing is to carry lots of plasters and antiseptic cream and liquids. In the Pacific, any cut you get walking on the reef or snorkelling will turn septic. You must apply antiseptic and you must keep the cuts clean and dry.

When I sliced off my thumbnail at Ahe Atoll, in Polynesia, I had run out of antiseptic. I created some by boiling water with salt and bleach in it, and soaked my thumb in the mixture. It was painful. I also started taking penicillin and managed to prevent any infection.

PRESCRIPTION REMEDIES.

Before I left, I got the pharmacist at home to make up a list of things I should take with me, and he got the doctor to issue them on the basis of a private prescription. They included remedies for earache, urinary tract infections, jelly fish stings, dental abscesses, chest infections, etc, and some very strong pain killers. The only thing I used was the antibiotic for dental problems.

Most of the stuff expired after about three years, and in the Caribbean I met up with a French doctor who was also sailing and who kindly went through my medicine box and re-prescribed a whole lot of stuff which the chemist ashore happily supplied.

INNOCULATIONS.

Before I left I got inoculations for Yellow Fever, Polio, Tetanus, Hepatitis A and Typhoid. I was never asked to show the certificates, but it was good to know that I had the protection.

DENTAL STUFF.

Before I left, my dentist did her best to make my teeth bullet proof, but suggested that there were three which it might be better to remove. Always keen to put off unpleasant experiences, I decided to keep them. When I got back four years later, I had left one in Vanuatu, one in Australia and one in South Africa. She was kind enough not to say anything...

THE LAST WORD.

I was unable to get any medical insurance before I left, and I sailed uninsured throughout the trip. During the voyage I needed medical, and, or, dental assistance in the

Caribbean, the Marquesas, New Zealand, Vanuatu, Darwin and South Africa. On every occasion I was impressed by the kindness of the people who helped me and by the very high standard of the care I received from them.

24. STAYING IN TOUCH.

When I started reading books about cruising and ocean voyaging it was common to read about yachts on ocean passages coming into sight of a ship and hoisting the code flags for their call sign, along with the letters, MIK, which if my memory serves, meant "Please report me to Lloyds of London". Legendary French sailor Bernard Moitessier used to place a written message in a plastic film container and fire it on to the deck or the bridge of a passing ship with his catapult.

The advent of the internet and email has made the world a very small place and communication, even from a small yacht at sea, is very easy.

SATELLITE PHONE.

I had an Iridium satellite phone, permanently installed at the chart table and operating through an external aerial mounted on the rail at the stern. I linked the phone to my laptop with a serial/USB converter cable, and after some difficulty, due in part to my own ineptitude, installed the necessary software to enable me to receive and send emails and download weather gribs via the satellite phone. Once I was used to it the system worked very well and used minimal power.

ADVANTAGES AND DISADVANTAGES.

The satellite telephone has one very big benefit, which is that, provided I have credit, I can contact anyone, at anytime from anywhere in the world. Better still, anyone in the family who has my number can contact me at any time if they need to. In the four years of my trip, I only used the phone for voice communication on a couple of occasions and no one ever called me. Perhaps there's a message there?

The disadvantage of the Iridium system is the cost. You buy minutes of credit in advance, and they have a use by date. You can manage usage by compressing emails, loading them into your outbox and then only opening the satellite connection once a day. When the connection is made, your outbox empties and incoming mail is received. The whole thing can be done in under a minute, but you must safeguard access by only releasing the boat's email address to those who need to have it, and to make sure they know that they should keep their messages brief and avoid attachments altogether. Photographs, etc, are completely out. If there is a big file attachment, and the link opens, your phone will keep downloading the attachment until it has been received, using up costly minutes, in return for which you possibly get a picture of someone's kitten.

You also need to disable automatic updates on the PC, or you will be using up even more of your precious minutes. You can always enable updates again once you are in port and on wifi.

SINGLE SIDE BAND RADIO.

American sailors love their SSB sets and they love talking to each other on them, possibly because in America you just buy the set, install it, get yourself a call sign and start talking.

Things are less simple in the UK When I was planning my trip I thought about having a transmitting SSB but I was put off by the cost of the set, the complexity of its installation and by the fact that here in the UK I would need to do a course and sit an exam in order to become licensed to operate it. I ended up buying a receive-only set which allowed me to listen to other boats and to receive weather forecasts from shore stations. Listening to the conversations between the other boats on their daily schedule was very useful, since each boat begins by reporting their position and giving a run-down of the weather they are experiencing. By plotting their positions and relating them to my own, I could build up a good picture of how a weather situation was developing.

ADVANTAGES AND DISADVANTAGES.

The big advantage of SSB communication is that it is free, and allows the boat to converse with others within range. Yachts on an Indian or Pacific ocean crossing have a daily schedule during which they exchange information and general chat. The radio schedule becomes a focal point of the day and can provide an important safety link between boats in range of each other. Some sailors like to 'hold hands' with those on other boats and their daily chats help them to do so.

There are a number of very experienced meteorologists around the world who maintain an overview of ocean weather conditions and run a daily SSB schedule with yachts on crossings. Most of these guys are incredibly helpful and have a real interest in what they are doing. On the Indian Ocean crossing I listened to Sam, in South Africa. I would send him an email every day or so, and he would include Beyond in his forecasts. He was spot on, and accurately predicted the timing of one very big depression which caused us all problems, alerting us to what we should expect on a daily basis. We met up when we got to Simonstown and it was a pleasure to share a meal and a few beers with him.

To my mind, the disadvantages of SSB are that an SSB set uses a lot of power when it is transmitting and the aerial has to be carefully insulated and may have to be tuned to get the best out of it. The set also has to be properly grounded, via a copper strip and a ground plate attached to the hull. The effectiveness and clarity of the signal is affected by atmospheric conditions. In the right conditions, communication over huge distances can be achieved, in poor conditions it can be very difficult at times. There is a certain amount of skill required and experienced operators will re-tune up and down the frequencies to get the best link under the conditions prevailing. SSB communication, is, of course, completely without privacy.

You can send and receive email via SSB, by the use of a modem, but that is another piece of equipment in the chain, and of course the success of the operation is subject to the same restrictions as that of the radio signal.

Although I would probably have enjoyed staying in touch with other boats by SSB, had I been able to transmit, I don't think I particularly missed being able to do so. Although I was on my own I never experienced a real need to talk to anyone when I was on passage and a lot of the radio chat between boats sounded pretty banal to me. Perhaps I am just not very sociable.

MOBILE PHONES.

Your mobile phone may work in some remote areas, but the chances are that if it does you will find yourself hit with some very high bills. I found the easiest way to get along was not to have a phone at all, or if I was in a situation where I needed one, such as during a refit where I needed to speak to suppliers, and so on, I would buy a cheap throw away phone locally with 'pay as you' go time on it. There were some very good deals available.

TIMES HAVE CHANGED.

Sailors on long term cruises are much less content to remain in isolation than they once were, and you will see boats select an anchorage on the strength of its phone signal, or cluster in one part of a bay because they can get a signal. In Mauritius a bunch of us were anchored in Grand Baie, a beautiful spot at the North end of the island. One of the boats discovered that if they anchored off a certain hotel they could hitch a free ride on its wifi, and soon the spot became crowded. The manager may have wondered what suddenly made the frontage of his hotel so popular.

Many cruisers seem intent on reproducing life ashore. I have seen catamarans with their own internal wifi nets, flat screen televisions, air conditioning and even dishwashers. I found that there was something quite liberating about doing without the convenience of a phone when in port. If I wanted to speak to another yacht nearby I would row over and speak to them, or possibly call on the VHF. Any emails I needed to send were sent in the evening, when once a day I would row ashore, get online, open my inbox and read whatever might be there then send off any mail I needed to send.

I had worked for years in an environment where I was in constant email touch with my organisation, and available pretty much twenty four hours a day at the end of a phone. For me, life on board was life on board. It was different, and all the more enjoyable for that.

25. RE-FIT...CRUISER TOWN.

Most cruising yachts will aim to haul out and refit every eighteen months or two years and many do so in New Zealand. The seasonal constraints of cruising sailing mean that most boats like to get out of the cyclone zone by the end of October and New Zealand offers cruising sailors the perfect place to dodge the storms, to access all the services they need, to re-fit and the opportunity to enjoy all that a summer in this wonderful country can offer.

Many head to Whangarei in the North Island about three hours up the coast from Auckland. The town straddles the banks of the Hatea river with its tree lined banks, boatyards, pontoon berths, slipways and wooden boathouses and plays host to over one hundred ocean cruising boats every summer.

It wasn't always like that. I first called there back in the mid-sixties on a pretty rough Glasgow registered cargo ship running phosphate down from the islands. We were berthed well down the river and there wasn't much worth going ashore for. Things have changed.

These days the ships berth miles away towards the open sea, where massive modern jetties enable the import of oil and the export of timber. But instead of fading, the town of Whangarei has adapted and right at its heart lies the Town Basin Marina, with pile and pontoon moorings, colonial style buildings, pubs, restaurants and easy access to supermarkets, chandlers, boat builders, engineers and every possible service a cruising yacht and its crew could wish for.

Every year, around November, like weary seabirds coming home to roost, ocean cruising boats begin to arrive from the North, to fold their wings, rest, relax and re-fit after months and months up amongst the islands.

If you are cruising in the Pacific you need to be pretty self-sufficient, and keeping the boat going can be challenging. The folk in the islands will generally do their best to help, but getting spares flown in from New Zealand, Australia or from the USA can be both difficult and expensive in terms of air freight and customs clearances. There are very few places where you can get work done in the islands and those where you can, such as the French islands like Tahiti or Raiatea are often frighteningly expensive. So work gets put off and many of the boats arriving in New Zealand have long worklists. There are boatyards in other North Island ports such as Opua, and of course in Auckland, but Opua is well North and a little isolated and whilst there is a high degree of expertise available in Auckland, that lovely city is the capital of New Zealand's superyacht business and prices reflect that.

The good folk of Whangarei were quick to recognise the potential market and revenue available from visiting cruising yachts. A very healthy marine business community has built up and the town offers everything the cruising yachtsman could wish for. Many of the marine businesses were started years ago by cruising people who arrived and somehow never left. Immigration rules must have been a lot less strict in those days! The town goes out of its way to attract cruising boats from the North, and there is healthy competition amongst the boatyards, engineers, sailmakers and chandlers, some of whom send advance guards up to the islands to secure re-fit business from the yachts before they start heading South.

With only my fifty year old memories of the place at the back of my mind, I wasn't sure of what I would find and I had no idea that such a well organised and friendly place lay waiting. From the moment I tied up alongside the Town Basin arrival berth I was made welcome and I soon realised that, almost by chance, I had landed in a sort of cruising sailors promised land.

Deep water cruising is certainly rewarding, and a very fulfilling experience, but after a year or so, you look forward to little bit of civilisation and in my case, to a little company. In New Zealand you will meet up with boats and sailors you may already have met months previously in various locations up the line and there is a great family atmosphere around the river in Whangarei as old friends are re-united, new friends made, and yarns spun.

On the technical side, there are five boatyards, including one which can haul out large catamarans, often a problem for multi-hull sailors. I doubt if there is anything you need on a boat that you cannot get done in New Zealand. It is generally agreed that if you stranded a New Zealander on an island, with a tree and a penknife, they would build a boat and get home, or possibly head further off. The whole atmosphere in the country is friendly and helpful. I find that when I am on my own with no one to talk things over with, problems tend to magnify themselves. Arriving in a place where you are surrounded by knowledgeable and helpful people, not only diminishes your problem, it brings on a pleasant feeling of relaxation.

The perfect interlude after months of ocean wandering.

A stopover in New Zealand often marks the half way point for boats from Europe which are going all the way round, and many of the boats arriving will be planning to cover thousands of miles more. You almost need to go over the boat all over again, just as you did when you first set out all those months ago. Remember the section on Wear and Tear? The difference this time is that you have all those miles, months and memories behind you. Your next re-fit might well be in South Africa, another wonderful stopover where you can get almost anything done but those ocean miles lie ahead, and the Indian Ocean has to be crossed. Take advantage of your time in New Zealand, rest, relax and re-fit. You and your boat may be more tired than you think.

26. JOURNEY'S END.

Well, there we are. If you have got this far you will, amongst other things, have survived heavy weather, calms, sail handling difficulties and electrical dilemmas. You will have planned your passage, arrived safely and anchored and may even now be enjoying your safe arrival drink.

I hope you have enjoyed the experience and that in reading what I have written you will be encouraged to sail further afield, and venture a little beyond your comfort zone. The advent of GPS, accurate weather forecasting, satellite telephones and email make doing so a far less daunting prospect than it once was.

Relatively low cost air travel and today's instant communication make the world a very small place, and to some extent it is swamped with travellers but it is still worth exploring. Doing so under sail will get you access to places unavailable to the conventional traveller, or only available to them at great expense.

Spending twenty four hours in a cramped and crowded aeroplane on an economy ticket to the other side of the world is an experience to be endured rather than enjoyed. Spending a year or so getting there under sail will provide personal satisfaction and lasting memories which you will treasure for the rest of your life.

If this book has one aim, it is to re-assure the reader that getting across the oceans is not difficult. The hardest part is probably making up your mind to go.

Stuart MacDonald, *At home in Scotland, May 2017.*

Lightning Source UK Ltd.
Milton Keynes UK
UKHW020737250420
362243UK00017B/1420